THE TWEEN GIRLS PUBERTY BIBLE

STRESS-FREE GUIDE TO EMBRACE YOUR
CHANGING BODY, PRACTICE SELF-CARE,
AND ENHANCE EMOTIONAL GROWTH TO
BECOME CONFIDENT GIRL IN JUST 15
MINUTES A DAY

INNERSPARKS

TABLE OF CONTENTS

INTRODUCTION

Welcome! I'm so glad you're here. I'm Innersparks, and I'm here to help you tackle this exciting time in your life head-on. Puberty is an incredible experience that each of us takes uniquely. Think of it as unlocking new levels in a game or growing wings and learning to fly. Like any adventure, there will be excitement, curiosity, confusion, and nervousness. It's all part of the process; those feelings are entirely normal.

You may feel overwhelmed with all the changes happening. Maybe you're excited or worried. Either feeling is okay. Many girls feel the same way. Puberty is a time when your body and emotions start to change, and it can be a lot to take in. But remember, you're not alone! This book is here to help guide you through it all, step by step.

So, what will you gain from reading this book? First, you'll learn about the changes happening in your body. We'll talk about everything from growth spurts to periods. You'll also

learn practical self-care tips, such as managing your skin and choosing the right hygiene products. Most importantly, you'll build confidence and emotional resilience. You'll learn to handle mood swings, deal with peer pressure, and celebrate your unique experience as it comes.

That's a lot to learn at once! But don't worry; this book is designed to be read in short, manageable segments. You only need to spend 15 minutes a day on it. This format will help you gradually build knowledge and confidence, without feeling like you have too much to handle at once.

Even better, each chapter features stories from girls just like you. You're not alone in your experiences, and there's always a way to overcome challenging times. You'll also get some practical tips and step-by-step guidance you can apply daily. This way, you'll always have a solution for any problems puberty throws your way.

Finally, the exercises in each chapter will help you wrap up what you've learned and reinforce your understanding. They also serve as great conversation starters with parents, guardians, or teachers, so you can start discussions about what you're going through and get the support you need.

So here we go! Let's start this fantastic adventure with an open mind and excitement for the changes ahead. This book is your companion, and it's ready to help you tackle puberty with confidence and positivity.

1. YOUR AWESOME PUBERTY ADVENTURE

One day, Lily noticed something different. Her favorite tee shirt felt tighter, and she suddenly wanted to cry for no reason. Feeling a mix of curiosity, confusion, and a little fear, Lily didn't know what was happening to her body or why she felt so emotional. She wondered if others felt the same way, and worried about whether her feelings were normal. She wasn't sure who she should talk to, or what she should do about how she was feeling. It all felt like too much, and to be honest, she just wanted to hide in her room from everyone.

If you've ever felt like Lily, you're not alone. Puberty can feel like a mysterious adventure full of twists and turns. But guess what? It's a natural and exciting part of growing up. You're totally normal if you feel mixed emotions during this time, and there are things that will help you feel better. Here, you'll learn the basics of puberty. This way, you can prepare for what's headed your way and have practical solutions ready for when you're feeling uncomfortable emotions about the changes puberty gives you. Let's get started by explaining what puberty is and how it works.

What is Puberty, Really?

Puberty is when your body changes from a child's to an adult's. Did you know that most girls start going through puberty between the ages of 8 and 13? This might sound surprising or scary, but it's a natural part of growing up. Imagine it like a caterpillar transforming into a butterfly. Just like that caterpillar, your body is going through its remarkable transformation. It's all powered by something called hormones. Hormones are chemicals that tell your body when to start these changes.

So, how do these hormones work? Well, there are two main hormones at work during puberty: estrogen and testosterone. Estrogen is mostly active in girls, while boys have more active testosterone. These hormones start working behind the scenes, causing all sorts of changes. For example, you might notice you're growing taller quickly, which is often called a growth spurt. Your body might also start developing curves. You'll probably see more hair growing in new places, like underarms and legs. Boys and girls go through these changes, but the timing and specific changes that occur can differ.

Let's break down these changes in a simple way. When estrogen in girls begins its work, it leads to breast development. This is when you might notice buds forming under your nipples. This is completely normal. Also, your hips

8

may get wider, which is preparing your body for the future of being a woman. Meanwhile, testosterone in boys causes their voices to deepen and facial hair to grow. They also experience growth spurts and muscle development. Both boys and girls will see changes in their skin, like increased oiliness, which can lead to pimples.

There are a lot of myths out there about puberty. One common myth is that puberty happens overnight. You might think you'll go to bed one day as a child, and wake up the next as an adult. Thankfully, this isn't true. Puberty is a gradual process that happens over several years. Another myth is that everyone goes through puberty at the same time. Some of your friends might start earlier, while others start later. This is also normal. If you're worried about starting puberty before or after all your friends, don't worry. Everyone will catch up with each other on their own time. It's part of what makes your body unique. Finally, some think puberty is only about physical changes, but it's also about emotional growth. You'll find your feelings and moods changing, too.

It's important to understand that everyone's experience with puberty is different. Your experience is your own, and there's no right or wrong way to go through it. Some people might feel more emotional changes before they see physical ones. Others might grow taller first and then notice other changes.

For example, Sarah noticed she was growing taller long before she got her first period. She felt out of place because her friends were experiencing different changes at different times. Meanwhile, Sarah's friend Emma started developing breasts before she noticed any height change. Both were perfectly normal experiences.

Understanding these changes and knowing they are normal can help you feel more confident. Remember, the feelings

9

of curiosity, confusion, and excitement are all part of the process. You're not alone in this. If you ever feel unsure, talking to a trusted adult can help. They can provide reassurance and answer any questions you might have (Reese, 2024a). We'll talk more about having conversations about puberty with others later in the book, so be on the lookout for it.

Embracing Your Puberty Experience: It's Unique!

Your experience with puberty is special because it's yours. Imagine a garden full of flowers. Each one blooms in its own time and in its own way. Just like those flowers, no two people experience puberty the same way. Some girls might start seeing changes earlier, while others might notice them later. It's all normal and part of what makes you uniquely you. Embrace these changes, and remember, your experience is your own.

Self-acceptance is a big part of feeling good during this time. It's important to love your changing body and appreciate what it can do. Positive self-talk can help a lot. You can do this by looking in the mirror and saying things like, "I am strong," or "I am beautiful just the way I am." Another great activity is to write down three things you love about yourself. These could be physical traits, like your curly hair or bright smile, or qualities like your kindness or sense of humor. Keep this list somewhere you can see it often. It's a great reminder of how amazing you are (Gupta, 2022).

Patience and self-compassion are also great to have during puberty. Changes don't happen overnight. They come gradually, and taking them one day at a time is essential. Be kind to yourself during this time of change. If you ever feel overwhelmed, remember asking for help is okay. Talk to a trusted adult or write down your feelings in a journal. This can help you process what you're going through (Moore

2019).

In the same way, you wouldn't rush a flower to bloom; don't rush yourself. Each stage of puberty has its beauty and significance. Celebrate your small victories and changes. Maybe you've noticed your hair getting thicker, or you've grown a few inches taller. These are milestones worth celebrating.

Remember, everyone's experience with puberty is different. Some girls might feel excited about the changes, while others might feel nervous. It's all okay. What matters is that you understand and accept yourself. Your puberty adventure is unique because it's yours.

Real-Life Stories From Girls Like You

Let's dive into some real-life stories from girls like you. Sometimes knowing how someone else got through a challenging situation gives you the power to overcome your challenges with confidence, too.

First, meet Mia. She was excited about getting her first period because her older sister had talked to her about it. She thought it was a rite of passage for being a teen. One day, it finally happened while she was at a family gathering. She felt a mix of excitement and pride. She quickly told her mom, who hugged her and congratulated her. That night, they even had a little celebration! Mia's experience was positive, and including her mom and sister in her experience made it easier to handle.

Next is Ava. When she started puberty, she got a lot of pimples on her face, which embarrassed her. She tried to hide her face with her hair and didn't want to look in mirror.

11

But, one day, she decided to talk to her mom, who took her to a dermatologist. The doctor helped Ava understand how to care for her skin, and her acne improved.

Now, let's hear about Zoe. Zoe's emotions were all over the place—one moment, she'd be super happy, and the next, she'd feel like crying. She didn't know how to handle all these mood swings and felt overwhelmed. Zoe started journaling and writing down her feelings, which helped her understand them better. She also talked to her school counselor, who taught her breathing exercises and relaxation techniques to use when feeling emotional.

Then, there's Emily. She felt left out because her friends were developing faster than she was. She was the last one

in her friend group to get her period and grow taller, which made her feel like she didn't fit in. Feeling a bit left out, Emily talked to her older cousin, who told her that everyone develops at their own pace and that it's okay to be different. Emily also joined a sports team, where she made new friends and started feeling more confident.

Each of these girls learned something important. Mia shows that having a positive attitude can make changes easier, and Ava reminds us that seeking help, like talking to a doctor, can help solve problems. At the same time, Zoe teaches us that finding ways to cope with emotions, like journaling or relaxation techniques, can improve things. And Emily demonstrated that getting support and joining new activities can help you feel more confident, even when you feel different from others.

These stories aren't just about the challenges of puberty; they're about finding solutions. These girls exemplify that while puberty can be challenging, it's also a time to learn and grow. You can go through this time confidently and positively by finding comfort in shared experiences, talking to trusted adults, and taking care of yourself.

Setting Goals for Your Puberty Experience

Setting goals can be a powerful way to get through puberty. I like to think of goals as small steps that help you manage the changes and emotions you're experiencing. One effective way to set goals is by using the SMART framework. Your goals should be Specific, Measurable, Achievable, Relevant, and Timebound. For example, instead of saying, "I want to feel better," you might set a goal to drink eight glasses of water daily for a week. This goal is specific because it tells you exactly what to do. It's also measurable because you can count the glasses. It's achievable because it's a realistic goal for the average person. It's relevant and time-bound as well because staying hydrated helps you feel better, and you have a one-week limit.

Another great example is practicing positive self-talk daily. You could set a goal to say three positive things about yourself every morning for the next two weeks. This goal is specific, measurable, achievable, relevant, and time-bound. By breaking your goals into smaller, manageable steps, you will make them easier to achieve.

Self-reflection is another big part of goal setting. Take a moment to think about what you want to achieve or improve. Ask yourself questions like, "What do I want to feel more confident about?" or "What new habits do I want to develop?" Maybe you want to feel more confident speaking in front of others. Or perhaps you want to start a new hobby like

drawing. Reflecting on these questions helps you understand what is important to you and sets a clear path for your goals.

To help you with this process, I've included some practical tools. You'll find a helpful goal-setting worksheet below that will guide you through setting your SMART goals. Writing down your goals and tracking your progress will help you stay focused and motivated. It's also a great way to see how far you've come and visualize what you want to achieve.

Goal-Setting Worksheet: Create Your SMART Goals

This worksheet will help you create and track your SMART goals (Specific, Measurable, Achievable, Relevant, Time-bound). Use this to stay focused and motivated as you work toward your goals.

1. What is Your Goal?
Write down what you want to achieve. Be clear and specific about what you want to do.
- Example: "I want to start drinking more water."

2. Is Your Goal SMART?
Check if your goal meets the SMART criteria:
- Specific: Is your goal clear and detailed?
Example: "I will drink eight glasses of water every day."
- Measurable: Can you measure or track your progress?
Example: "I will keep track of how many glasses of water I drink daily."
- Achievable: Is your goal realistic and something you can do?
Example: "Drinking eight glasses of water is realistic for me because I can keep a water bottle with me."
- Relevant: Does your goal matter to you and fit your current needs?

Example: "Drinking more water will help me stay healthy and feel better."
- Time-bound: When do you want to reach this goal?
Example: "I will stick to this goal for the next two weeks."

Write down how you can make your goal SMART.

3. Write Your SMART Goal:
Now that you've broken it down, put it all together.
- Example: "I will drink eight glasses of water daily for the next two weeks to stay healthy and feel better."

4. Track and Reflect on Your Progress:
Use the table on the next page to keep track of how you're doing. You can add checkmarks or write notes to help you stay motivated.
Ask yourself the following questions and write down your answers.
- How did you feel while working on this goal?
- What challenges did you face. How did you overcome them?
- What did you learn from this experience?

5. Celebrate Your Success:
Write down one way you will reward yourself when you reach your goal!
- Example: "When I reach my goal, I'll treat myself to a fun movie night with friends."

As you work toward your goals, remember to celebrate your small wins. For example, if you reach your goal of drinking more water, reward yourself with something special. This could be a movie night with friends or getting that new book you've wanted. Sharing your success with friends or family can also feel good. When you tell someone about your achievements, you celebrate and inspire others to set their own goals.

DAY	DID I REACH MY GOAL?	MY NOTES AND THOUGHTS
DAY 1		
DAY 2		
DAY 3		
DAY 4		
DAY 5		

You can also create a reward system to stay motivated. To do this, make a chart and place a sticker on it each time you reach your goal for the day. Once you fill a row with stickers, treat yourself to something small, like a fun outing or one of your favorite snacks. Seeing your progress in front of you can be really encouraging.

Remember, setting goals isn't just about achieving something huge. It's about making small, positive changes that help you grow. Each step you take brings you closer to feeling more confident and in control. It's okay if some goals take longer to reach than others. Don't be hard on yourself if you don't reach a goal immediately. Take a moment to reflect on your learning and make a new plan, if necessary, to keep moving forward (Bell, n.d.).

As you read this book, keep your goals in mind. Use the tools given to you in this chapter to help you stay on track. Celebrate both your big and small milestones, and always be kind to yourself. Puberty is full of changes, but you can confidently get through it with clear goals and a positive attitude. Next, you'll learn more about how puberty will gradually change your body and how you can prepare for it. You'll also learn some helpful tips for choosing your first bra and keeping your confidence high when these changes happen.

2. PUBERTY 101
WHAT'S HAPPENING TO ME?

To start things off, imagine you're sitting in class, and suddenly, your legs feel cramped in your chair. You stretch out, realizing you're a bit taller than you were last month. Then, you glance at your friends and notice they're growing, too. This is one of the first signs of puberty. Your body is changing, and it can feel like a whirlwind. But don't worry; understanding what's happening can make this time exciting and less confusing. Throughout this chapter, you'll learn more about how puberty affects the body and ways you can keep yourself feeling comfortable and confident during this transition.

What's Happening to My Body?

During puberty, your body goes through many changes. One of the main changes you'll notice is growth spurts. This is when you suddenly grow taller, and your limbs lengthen. You might feel awkward adjusting to your new height, but this is a natural part of growing up. Your body is getting stronger

and preparing for adulthood. Another significant change is the development of secondary sexual characteristics. For girls, this includes the growth of breasts and the widening of hips. You'll also start to see more body hair in new places, like your underarms and the pubic area. This might initially feel strange, but it's just your body's way of maturing.

Your body's composition will also change. For example, you might notice you're gaining weight in new places, like your hips and thighs. This is all part of your body's development. Your muscles will also grow stronger, and your body will look more like a young adult's. It's common to feel growing pains in your legs and arms during this time as well. These pains are usually mild and go away on their own. Eating a balanced diet and getting enough sleep can help your body better handle these changes.

Additionally, you'll likely find that your skin is starting to change as you enter puberty. You might find that your skin becomes oilier, and you start to get pimples. This is because your oil glands are becoming more active. Pimples can appear on your face, back, and chest.

Almost everyone deals with acne at some point during puberty, so you're definitely not alone. Keeping your skin clean with a gentle cleanser and trying not to pick at pimples can help, but remember, it's a normal part of this phase. If your acne worsens, you can also talk to a dermatologist, a doctor who specializes in skin care, for advice on managing it. Understanding these changes can make puberty feel less overwhelming. Your body is doing exactly what it's supposed to do, even if it feels strange sometimes. Embrace these changes and know that you're not alone (Reese, 2024a).

Hormones—The Magic Messengers

Hormones are tiny chemical messengers that tell your body when it's time to start changing. They trigger many of the changes you experience during puberty and play a significant

Estrogen   Testosterone

role in your emotions.

Remember estrogen, one of the main hormones for girls, from Chapter 1? It acts like an orchestra conductor, telling different parts of your body when to start playing their part. When estrogen increases, it signals your breasts to start developing. This begins with small bumps under your nipples called breast buds. Over time, these buds grow, and your breasts get larger. Estrogen also tells your hips to widen, so you might notice your body taking on a curvier shape. Estrogen helps regulate your menstrual cycle as well. Testosterone is another essential hormone. While it's more active in boys, girls have it, too. Testosterone helps muscles and bones to grow. It also plays a role in developing body hair.

Growth hormone (GH) is another key player in puberty. This hormone is responsible for those sudden growth spurts you might experience. It tells your bones to grow longer and

your muscles to get stronger. Growth hormone works behind the scenes, making sure your body grows in the right way as you grow and change. They send signals to different parts of your body to tell them when to start developing.

Hormones don't just change your body; they also affect your emotions. You might notice that you feel happy one moment and sad or agitated the next. This is because estrogen and testosterone can influence your mood and make you feel more emotional. You might experience mood swings when your feelings change quickly. Understanding that these feelings are normal can help you cope with them. It's important to remember that your emotions are valid, and it's okay to feel different from one day to the next.

By learning about hormones, you can better understand what's happening in your body and feel more in control. Talking to a trusted adult can also provide more clarity and support if you have questions or feel unsure. Remember, everyone goes through these changes, and you're not alone in your experience (Discover, 2021).

Managing Growth Spurts

Growth spurts are when your body suddenly grows taller and your arms and legs get longer. These spurts usually happen in waves, so you develop a lot over a few months and only grow a little for a while. For most girls, growth spurts start around ages 9 to 11 years old and can last until your late teens.

During a growth spurt, you'll likely notice you're outgrowing your clothes and shoes faster than usual. This might feel strange, but it's a sign that your body is doing what it should. Going through a growth spurt can feel like a rollercoaster.

Sometimes, you might experience growing pains, which are

aches in your legs and arms. These typically happen at night and can be uncomfortable. You might also find that your favorite jeans or shoes suddenly don't fit. One day, they're perfect, and the next, they're too short or tight. This can be frustrating, but it's all part of growing up. Your body is stretching and changing, and it's normal to feel awkward while this happens.

You can try doing some gentle stretches before bed to make growing pains more comfortable. Stretching can help ease the tightness in your muscles and make you feel better. Eating healthy foods is also essential. Make sure that you get lots of vitamins and minerals from fruits, vegetables, and whole grains to help your body grow strong. And don't forget to get enough sleep. Your body grows a lot while you're sleeping, so it's important to rest.

Keeping track of your growth can be fun, too. You can start a growth chart where you mark your height every few months. It's cool to see how much you're changing, and it gives you a way to celebrate your milestones. You might also notice when you finally catch up to your older sister or grow taller than your mom. It's exciting and worth celebrating!

Growth spurts are a big part of puberty. Even though they might make you feel awkward sometimes, they're a sign that your body is growing and developing just like it should. Embrace these changes and remember that everyone goes through them. You're not alone (Reese, 2024b).

Breast Development—What to Expect

One of the significant changes you'll notice during puberty is breast development. It happens in different stages, called the Tanner stages. In Stage 1, there aren't any visible signs of development yet. Your chest still looks the same as it did when you were younger. Then comes Stage 2, when you start

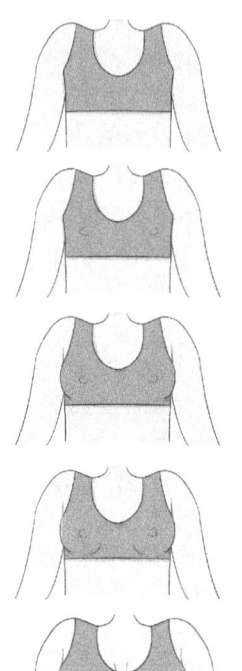

to feel breast buds under your nipples. These small lumps might feel tender or sore but don't worry. That's normal!

Your breasts start to get rounder and fuller in Stage 3. You might also notice that the areola (the darker skin around your nipple) is getting bigger. By Stage 4, your breasts continue to grow, and the areola becomes more noticeable.

Sometimes, the nipple and areola can form a small bump above the rest of your breast. This means your body is still developing. Finally, in Stage 5, your breasts reach their adult size and shape. They stop growing at this point, and each girl reaches these stages at her own pace, so don't worry if you're developing faster or slower than your friends.

During breast development, you might feel some new sensations. Tenderness and soreness are common, especially if you bump into something or lie on your stomach. You might also notice some itching as your skin stretches to make room for your growing breasts. Sometimes, you might even see stretch marks. These red or purple lines appear as your skin stretches, and they usually fade over time.

It's also totally normal for your breasts to grow at different rates. One breast might be a little bigger than the other for a while, but this uneven development typically evens out as you continue growing.

Every girl's body is different, and that includes breast development. Some of your friends might develop earlier or later than you, and some might have larger or smaller breasts. These differences are all completely normal. Breasts

24

come in many shapes and sizes, and they're all beautiful in their own way. It's important to remember that your body is changing at its own pace, so try not to compare yourself to others. Try to focus on your experience. Your body knows what it's doing (Wisner, 2023).

Choosing Your First Bra

As your body changes, you might notice your chest growing and feeling differently. This is normal! A bra can help support your growing breasts and make you feel more comfortable, especially during sports and while running or jumping. A bra can also boost your confidence because you will feel more comfortable in your skin when you have the proper support.

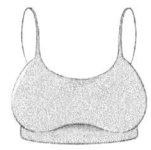
Training bra

There are lots of different types of bras that are great for beginners. One option is a training bra, which gives light support and is perfect for when your breasts are just starting to develop. Training bras are super simple and often look like a crop top, so they're a nice, easy place to start. Another option is a sports bra. These are made to give you extra support during gym class or sports practice. They're great if you're running around or playing sports like soccer. And then there are bralettes, which are comfy, cute, and don't have any underwire. They're perfect for everyday wear and come in fun styles and colors.

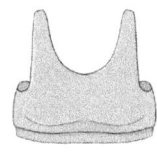
Sports bra

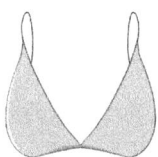
Bralette

Finding the right size is essential. A bra that's too tight will feel uncomfortable, and one that's too loose won't give you the support you need.

Here's how you can measure yourself for a bra:
- First, measure your band size by wrapping a soft measuring tape around your rib cage, just under your

breasts. Make sure the tape is snug but not too tight, then write down that number.

- Next, measure your bust size by wrapping the tape around the fullest part of your chest. Again, ensure it's not too tight, and write that number down, too.
- Now, subtract your band size from your bust size. The difference will tell you your cup size. For example, if the difference is one inch, you're likely an A cup; if it's two inches, you're probably a B cup; and so on.

Shopping for your first bra can be fun! Try different styles to see what feels good for you. Look for a bra with adjustable straps and closures to make sure it fits just right and can be adjusted as your body changes. It's also a good idea to choose soft and breathable fabrics, such as cotton, because they're comfortable and easy to take care of. Don't hesitate to ask for help if you're unsure about anything. Stores often have friendly staff to help you find the right size and style. Most importantly, remember that finding the right bra is about what makes you feel comfortable and confident. Whether you prefer a training bra, sports bra, or bralette, it's all about what feels best for your body (Raising Children 101, 2022).

Understanding Body Odor and Sweat

You might notice a new smell from your underarms or feet one day. This is body odor, and it happens because your sweat glands become more active as your body matures. There are two types of sweat glands: eccrine glands and apocrine glands.

- **Eccrine glands** make sweat that is mostly water and salt, and they help cool your body. You'll notice this type of sweat when you exercise or it's hot outside.
- **Apocrine glands**, which start working during puberty, are found in places like your underarms. The sweat from these glands is thicker and contains proteins and fats. When this

Apocrine gland   Eccrine gland

sweat mixes with the bacteria on your skin, it can cause body odor. You might notice this kind of sweat more when you're nervous or stressed, like before a big test or an important event.

Knowing how your body works can help you plan. For example, you might use extra deodorant before a party or keep a spare shirt in your bag if you're worried about sweating too much during the day.

Managing body odor might seem tricky initially, but following good hygiene habits is pretty simple. Start by showering every day, especially after gym class or playing sports. When showering, use gentle soap to clean your skin, and pay special attention to cleaning your underarms and feet. You also need to apply deodorant or antiperspirant. Deodorants help cover up the smell, while antiperspirants help reduce how much you sweat. You might need to try a few different products to find the one that works best for you.

Wearing clothes made from breathable fabrics can also help. Cotton allows your skin to breathe and keeps sweat from sticking to your body. This prevents body odor because sweat can get trapped if you wear tight or synthetic clothes, and

27

this can make the smell stronger.

Even with good hygiene, sometimes you might feel like you're sweating too much or that your body odor is more potent than your friends'. You might wonder, "Is it normal to sweat so much?" The answer is yes! Everyone sweats, and some people sweat more than others. You'll naturally sweat more if it's a hot day or you've been active. That's just your body's way of cooling down.

If you're worried about the smell, remember it's completely normal. Your body is undergoing many changes, and it's taking time to adjust. If you ever feel like regular deodorant isn't working, don't hesitate to talk to your parent or a doctor. They can recommend stronger products or advise you on how to manage them.

Addressing concerns about body odor and sweat early on will help you feel more confident. Keep practicing good hygiene, and don't be afraid to ask for help if you need it. Your body is amazing and does so much for you. Taking care of it helps you feel your best daily (Krisch, 2022).

You'll learn more about how you can support your incredible body during puberty in the next chapter. You'll find out more about managing pimples, body hair, and weight changes. All while figuring out how to embrace your new body for the beautiful and unique one that it is.

3. BODY MAKEOVER
THE ULTIMATE
TRANSFORMATION

Have you ever woken up one morning and looked in the mirror to see a small pimple on your forehead? You might have felt surprised, annoyed, or even a little worried. This is a common experience during puberty. Your skin is going through changes, just like the rest of your body, and they can sometimes make you feel self-conscious. Understanding what's happening can help you take better care of your skin and feel more confident. In this chapter, you'll learn more about how your skin, weight, and body hair can change during puberty. You'll also get some helpful tips and tricks for managing these changes to keep you feeling cool and confident. Let's get started by finding out how you can keep those pesky pimples at bay.

Skin Changes: From Pimples to Glowing Skin

Acne is one of the most common things that happens during puberty, so if you notice pimples popping up, you're not alone. Acne happens because hormonal changes in your body cause your skin to produce extra oil. When this oil mixes with dead

skin cells and bacteria, it can clog your pores, which can lead to pimples, blackheads, or whiteheads. You might first notice acne on your face, but it can also show up on your back and chest and make those areas feel bumpy or sore.

Having acne can feel frustrating, but there are things you can do to manage it. Creating a skincare routine is one of the best ways to care for your skin during puberty. Start by cleaning your face gently twice daily. You can do this once in the morning and once before bed. I would use a mild cleanser that's not too harsh on your skin. Look for "non-comedogenic" cleansers. This term means that the product won't clog your pores.

After you wash your face, it's super important to moisturize. Even if your skin feels oily, using moisturizer helps keep your skin balanced. Choose a lightweight, oil-free moisturizer that won't make your skin greasy but will still give it the hydration it needs.

Acne can sometimes make you feel self-conscious, but everyone goes through it at some point, especially during puberty. It's just another sign that your body is growing and changing. If you ever feel frustrated with your acne or it bothers you a lot, you can always talk to a parent or doctor. They can help you find the best way to care for your skin.

Spot treatments can also be beneficial when you want to target a specific pimple. These treatments usually contain benzoyl peroxide or salicylic acid, which reduces redness and swelling and will make the pimple go away faster. Remember to apply a small amount directly to the pimple and be patient. Be gentle with your skin. Don't scrub or pick at your pimples, even if it's tempting. Picking at them can make things worse and might leave scars.

Healthy habits can also help keep your skin clear. For example, drinking plenty of water is excellent for your skin because it helps keep your skin hydrated and flushes out the bad stuff. You can also try eating lots of fruit and vegetables. These are packed with vitamins and minerals that help your skin stay healthy, and they will help you recover from breakouts faster.

Another good habit is to avoid touching your face with your hands. Your hands can carry bacteria and oil, leading to more pimples if they transfer to your skin. Also, if you feel stressed out, like before a big test or when dealing with many emotions, try doing things that help you relax. Stress can worsen acne, so yoga, meditation, or taking deep breaths can help you feel calmer and keep your skin happier.

Sometimes, people need something more than the acne treatments that can be bought from the store, especially if their acne lasts for a long time or is really severe. If that happens, seeing a dermatologist might be a good idea. They can give you more potent treatments, like special creams or medications, to help with stubborn pimples. If you have other skin problems, like rashes or dry skin, a dermatologist can help with those, too.

Skincare Routine Checklist

Creating a skincare routine can feel overwhelming, but breaking it down into simple steps can make it easier. Here's a checklist to help you get started:
1. **Cleanse**: Use a gentle cleanser twice a day, morning and night.
2. **Moisturize**: Apply a non-comedogenic moisturizer after cleansing.

3. **Spot Treat**: Use spot treatments on individual pimples as needed.
4. **Hydrate**: Drink plenty of water throughout the day.
5. **Eat Well**: Include fruits and vegetables in every meal.
6. **Hands Off**: Avoid touching your face to reduce bacteria transfer.
7. **Relax**: Find ways to manage stress, like yoga or meditation.

Finding what works best for your skin might take some time, but with patience and proper care, you'll feel more confident in no time! Remember, your skin is unique, just like you. Embrace these changes and take care of your skin with love and patience. Everyone goes through this, and you're not alone (Dr. Zenovia, 2021).

Hair Everywhere! What to Do About It

One day, you might notice tiny hairs growing in places where there weren't any before. This is normal! Your body is getting signals from hormones to start growing hair in new areas, like under your arms, on your legs, and in your pubic area. This happens because your body is maturing. Believe it or not, hair has an important job. It helps protect your skin from friction, like when your clothes rub against you. It also helps your body sense things, like when a bug crawls on you. Even the hair in your nose is helpful because it filters out dust and keeps your nose clean.

When it comes to managing body hair, there are many options. How you want to manage it is up to you. Shaving is one of the quickest and easiest methods. You can do it at home. Shaving cuts hair at the surface, so it may grow back fast. This is okay, though. It's not abnormal to find yourself needing to shave every few days during puberty.

Another option is waxing, which pulls the hair out from the root. This means it takes longer to grow back, so you don't have to do it as often. However, waxing can be painful and, sometimes, causes redness or irritation. If you remove your body hair, do it safely. Using clean, sharp razors can help prevent cuts and infections. Dull razors can cause nicks and lead to ingrown hairs. It's important to always shave in the direction of hair growth and use shaving cream or soap to reduce friction. After removing hair, moisturize your skin to keep it soft and prevent dryness. Look for gentle, fragrance-free lotions that won't irritate your skin. Waxing can also harm your skin if not done properly. Wax that's too hot can burn your skin. Waxing improperly can lead to ingrown hairs as well. It's a good idea to get help from a parent, guardian, or another trusted adult when shaving or waxing for the first time.

If you don't like the idea of shaving or waxing, there are depilatory creams. These creams dissolve the hair at the surface, making it easy to wipe away. But be careful; some people can have skin reactions to these creams. It's always a good idea to test a small skin patch first.

There are also more natural methods like sugaring and threading. Sugaring uses a sticky paste made from sugar, lemon, and water to remove hair, and it's less painful than waxing. Meanwhile, threading uses a thin piece of thread to pull out hair, and it's great for small areas like your eyebrows. Both methods can cause irritation but are generally gentle on your skin.

Deciding whether or not to remove body hair is up to you. Some people like to remove it, and others don't. Both options are completely okay. There's no right or wrong answer. The most important thing is that you feel comfortable and confident. Remember, body hair is entirely natural. It's normal to have it, and it's normal to remove it if you want to. Different cultures and societies have different ideas about body hair. In some places, it's common to remove body hair,

and in others, it's not as important. But what matters the most is how you feel about your body. Embrace your choices and know that whatever you decide is right for you. Always remember to respect others' choices about their bodies, too.

Body Hair Removal Guide

Choosing the proper hair removal method can seem overwhelming, but it doesn't have to be. Here's a guide to help you decide:

- **Shaving**: Quick and easy but needs frequent upkeep. Great for legs and underarms.
- **Waxing**: Longer-lasting results but can be painful. It is ideal for larger areas like legs.
- **Depilatory Creams**: Easy to use but may cause skin reactions. Suitable for quick hair removal.
- **Sugaring**: Natural and less painful than waxing. Suitable for almost any body part.
- **Threading**: Precise and great for small areas like eyebrows.

Each method has its pros and cons. Consider your skin type, pain tolerance, and how often you want to remove your body hair. If you're unsure, try different techniques to see what works best for you.

Understanding why body hair grows and knowing your options for managing it can help you feel more in control. Whether you remove your hair or let it grow, the most important thing is feeling comfortable in your skin. Talking to a trusted adult can provide more guidance and support if you have any worries or questions. Everyone's experience with body hair is different, and that's okay! Embrace what feels suitable for you and care for your skin with love and care (Miller, 2018).

Dealing with Weight Changes

As you go through puberty, you might notice that your weight is changing. During puberty, hormones work hard, and this can change how your body carries weight. For instance, you might find that you're gaining weight in places like your hips, thighs, and belly. This is your body's way of getting ready for adulthood, so there's no need to worry if you notice these changes.

You might also find yourself feeling hungrier than usual. That's because your body needs extra energy to handle all the growth it's going through. Have you ever had a day when you just felt like eating everything in sight? That's your body asking for more fuel. This can also happen during growth spurts when you grow taller very quickly. It's common to gain weight before a growth spurt and then slim down as you get taller.

Another thing to remember is that your body's composition (the way it's made up of muscle, fat, and bone) changes during puberty, too. You might gain more muscle during puberty, making you weigh more, even if you don't look much bigger. Girls also tend to gain more fat in their hips and thighs, which is a natural part of growing into a woman's body.

Maintaining healthy eating habits is important during this time. Focus on eating nutritious foods that give your body the energy it needs by including a variety of food groups in your meals. Fruits, vegetables, whole grains, and lean proteins are all important.

Here's a breakdown of what each food group does for you:
- **Fruits and Vegetables**: These are packed with vitamins, minerals, and fiber that help keep your skin clear, your immune system strong, and your energy levels steady.

Mix half of your plate with fruits and veggies at each meal. Whether it's a handful of berries with breakfast or carrot sticks with lunch, they're easy to include in your day.

- **Whole Grains**: Foods like brown rice, whole wheat bread, and oatmeal give you long-lasting energy. Whole grains are also rich in fiber, which helps with digestion and keeps you feeling full longer. Swapping out white bread or pasta for whole-grain versions is a small change that makes a big difference.
- **Lean Proteins**: Protein helps build and repair muscles, which is especially important as your body changes. Chicken, fish, eggs, beans, and nuts are excellent protein sources. You don't need a huge amount. Just a serving with each meal will help keep you strong.
- **Dairy or Dairy Alternatives**: Foods like milk, yogurt, and cheese (or fortified plant-based alternatives) are essential for bone health. They provide calcium and vitamin D, which help your bones stay strong as you grow.

Avoid fad diets or extreme eating restrictions. These can be harmful and don't provide the nutrients that you need. Listen to your hunger cues. Eat when you're hungry and stop when you're full. Eating mindfully helps you enjoy your food and recognize when you've had enough.

Staying active is also crucial to feeling good and managing your weight. Find physical activities that you enjoy. Dancing, swimming, and team sports are all fun ways to stay active. Exercise is beneficial because it can improve your mood, help you sleep better, and give you more energy. Set realistic fitness goals for yourself. Maybe you want to join a sports team or go for a walk every day. Whatever you choose, make sure that it's something you enjoy and can stick with.

Keep a positive body image regardless of weight changes. Appreciate your body for what it can do. Your body allows you to run, jump, dance, and play. Focus on these abilities rather than how your body looks. Avoid comparing yourself to your peers or images you see in the media. Everyone's body is different, and that's what makes each of us unique. Remember, your body is fantastic and doing what it needs to do (Spitza, 2016).

Celebrating Your Unique Body Shape

Your body is unique, just like you. Every girl goes through changes during puberty, but those changes happen differently for everyone. Some girls might get taller and leaner, while others might start to develop curves. There's no one way that bodies should look. Embracing body diversity means celebrating that all bodies are different and beautiful in their own way. Whether you're tall, short, curvy, or slim, your body is perfect just as it is.

Building confidence in your body starts with wearing clothes that make you feel comfortable and happy. Maybe you have a favorite dress that makes you feel like you can conquer anything, or you feel the most comfortable relaxing in a cozy hoodie. No matter what types of clothes are your favorite, wearing outfits that fit you well and make you feel good will help boost your confidence.

Surrounding yourself with positive people who make you feel good about yourself is important as well. Spend time with friends who lift you and family members who support you. Being around people who make you feel confident and loved helps you build a positive body image.

Unfortunately, people sometimes hurt others by making negative comments about them or body-shaming them. But remember, those comments say more about the person making them than they do about you. If someone says something hurtful, ignore it and focus on what you love about yourself. Maybe you love how strong your legs are

37

from playing soccer or how great your hair looks in a ponytail; whatever it is, remind yourself of those things when met with mean comments.

If you feel comfortable, you can also speak up when someone body-shames you or someone else. Let them know that everyone's body is different, and that's okay. Being kind and accepting of others and yourself is what really matters. You deserve to feel good about your body. Finding supportive friends and family who accept you for who you are can make all the difference.

Sometimes, the media promotes inaccurate body standards. Many pictures in magazines and on social media are edited or filtered to make people look different. For example, photo editing can make someone's skin look super smooth or make their waist look smaller than it actually is in real life.

Knowing that these images are often edited will help remind you that they aren't always accurate, so you don't have to compare yourself to them. Remember, real beauty comes in all shapes, sizes, and forms.

One fun way to feel great about your body is by celebrating milestones when you feel proud of something your body has done. Try keeping a journal where you write about positive experiences with your body. For example, you ran your fastest time during gym class or felt confident in a new outfit. Writing these moments down helps you remember how strong and beautiful you are.

As you go through puberty, your body works hard to help you grow and develop. Embrace these changes with pride because they are part of the unique, amazing person you are becoming. Celebrate who you are and remember that there's no one else quite like you (Long, 2023).

4. PERIOD POWER
OWNING YOUR CYCLE

Imagine sitting in class and suddenly feeling a strange cramp in your lower belly. You're not sure what it is, but you've heard older girls talk about something called a period. You feel a mix of curiosity, worry, and maybe excitement. This moment is a sign that your body is starting to really change.

Understanding what's happening can help make those changes a lot less scary. Here, you'll learn everything that you need to know about periods, from how they work to what to expect in your first one. You'll even get some helpful tips for choosing between pads, tampons, and other period products. Let's begin with the best starting point possible, learning about what periods are and why they happen.

What is Menstruation?

Menstruation, commonly known as a period, is a natural process that happens as your body matures. To understand

39

the process better, let's break down the menstrual cycle. Your body has three key players in this cycle: the ovaries, the uterus, and hormones. The ovaries are small organs that store eggs. The uterus, also called the womb, is where a baby can grow if you ever become pregnant. Hormones are chemicals that send messages to your body, telling it what to do and when.

The menstrual cycle has four main stages, and it happens every month.

- **First Stage: Follicular Phase**
  This stage starts on the first day of your period and continues until the middle of your cycle. During this time, your body releases a particular chemical called follicle-stimulating hormone (FSH). This hormone tells your ovaries to get an egg ready to be released.

- **Second Stage: Ovulation**
  Ovulation usually happens in the middle of your cycle. This is when another hormone, luteinizing hormone (LH), tells your ovary to release a mature egg. The egg then travels down the fallopian tube.

- **Third Stage: Luteal Phase**
  After the egg is released, the ovary sends out hormones that help prepare the inside of your uterus by growing a thick lining in case the egg is fertilized. The ovary does this by forming a temporary thing called a corpus luteum.

- **Fourth Stage: Menstruation**
  If the egg doesn't meet sperm and isn't fertilized, the corpus luteum breaks down. When this happens, your body doesn't need the thick lining in your uterus anymore, so it sheds and leaves your body as blood. This is commonly called "getting your period."

What can you expect during your period? The duration of a period usually lasts between two and seven days. The flow of blood can vary from light to heavy. Some days, you might notice just a few spots of blood, while other days, the flow might be heavier. The color of menstrual blood can change.

It can be bright red, dark brown, or even pink. This is all

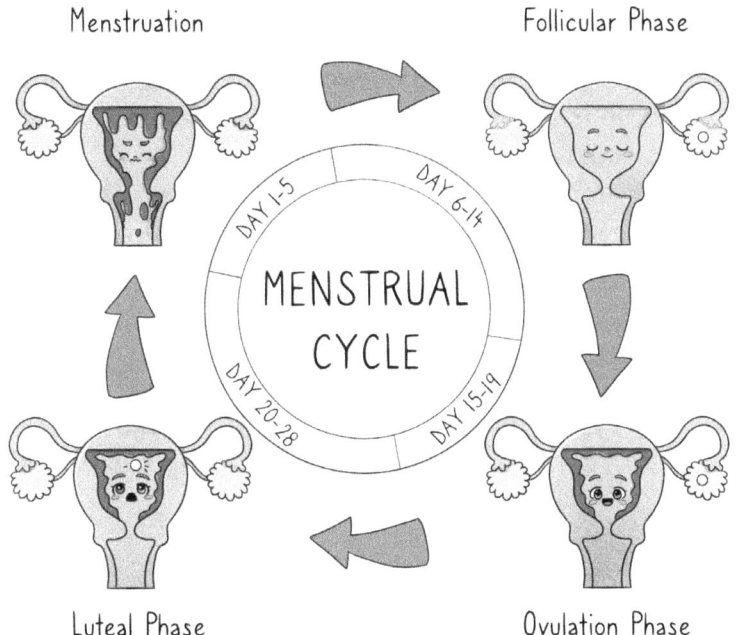

normal and part of the process.

During your period, you might notice some symptoms. One of the most familiar is cramps. Cramps happen because your uterus (the part of your body that sheds its lining during your period) tightens up to help get rid of the lining. You might feel these cramps in your lower belly, back, or thighs. It can feel uncomfortable, like a squeezing sensation, but it's normal.

Another symptom is bloating. You might feel like your stomach is puffier or tighter than usual. It can also make your clothes feel a little snug but don't worry, it's temporary. You might notice mood swings when your emotions are everywhere. One minute, you're happy, and the next minute, you feel sad or frustrated. This happens because of the hormonal changes your body is going through. It's common to experience this before your period and while it's happening.

It's important to know what is expected in a normal period and when you might need to ask for help. Typical symptoms include mild to moderate cramps, some bloating, and mood swings. But suppose you experience an extremely heavy flow, severe pain, or irregular cycles. In that case, it's a good idea to talk to a trusted adult or a doctor.

- Extremely heavy flow means you're going through more than one pad or tampon every hour for several hours in a row.
- Severe pain is when your cramps are so bad that you can't go to school or do your regular activities.
- Irregular cycles mean your periods are unpredictable, occurring much earlier or later than expected (Watson, 2018).

If you notice any of these symptoms above, you should reach out to an adult that you trust. It could mean you need some extra help managing your cycle, and that's okay. Periods aren't the same for everyone, and seeking help from a doctor when you need it will help keep your body healthy. It will also help you feel more comfortable.

Let me tell you about Sophie. When Sophie first got her period, she started experiencing some typical symptoms, like cramps and bloating. At first, the cramps weren't too bad. She would use a heating pad and rest for a while, which helped ease her discomfort. She also found that drinking water and avoiding salty snacks helped reduce the bloating. It wasn't always fun, but she got through her period with these simple tricks.

However, a few months after she started having periods, Sophie noticed that her cramps were getting worse. One day, the pain was so intense that she couldn't even get out of bed to go to school. She also noticed that she was going through more than one pad every hour, which was different from what she had experienced before. At first, she thought this might be normal, but after a couple of cycles like this, she realized something might be wrong.

Sophie started feeling nervous, so she decided to talk to her mom. She explained how severe the pain had become and how heavy her period flow was. Her mom was understanding and took her to see a doctor. The doctor reassured Sophie that it was a good thing that she had spoken up and asked for help. After discussing her symptoms, the doctor gave Sophie some medication to help with the cramps and suggested she start tracking her periods to keep an eye on her symptoms.

With the doctor's help, Sophie started feeling much better. The medication made her cramps more manageable, and by tracking her periods, she could prepare for when her period was about to start. She realized that asking for help wasn't something to be afraid of. It was important for her health. Now, Sophie feels more in control of her period and knows what to do when things don't feel right.
Don't hesitate to talk to a trusted adult if something with your period feels off. Like Sophie, you'll feel stronger and more confident, knowing you've taken the proper steps to care for yourself. You've got this! And you are not alone in handling this new part of your life.

Your First Period: What to Expect

You might start noticing some clues before your first period arrives. Don't worry; that's just your body's way of preparing you. One sign is vaginal discharge. This is a clear or white fluid you might see in your underwear, and it keeps everything clean and healthy. You might also feel cramps in your belly or have lower back pain. These cramps act as a little heads-up that your period might start soon.

Preparing for your first period can make the whole experience less stressful. Put together a little period kit. This kit could include a couple of pads, a spare pair of underwear, and wipes. Having these things ready will make you feel prepared no matter where you are when your period starts. Another helpful thing you can do is keep track of your body changes in a journal. Write down when you first notice things like breast development, growth spurts, or vaginal discharge.

Keeping track of these signs helps you understand when your period might come. It's also normal to feel a mix of emotions when your period first starts. You might feel excited, nervous, or a little scared. Take a few deep breaths if you start feeling overwhelmed. Many girls go through this during their first periods, and you're not alone (Villines, 2021). Here are a couple of stories from girls who have gone through their first periods.

Sarah got her first period while she was at school. She felt a cramp in her belly during math class and went to the bathroom. When she saw the blood, she felt a bit panicked. But then she remembered that her mom had told her to stay calm. Sarah took a deep breath, used the pad from her period kit, and went to the school nurse, who reassured her and called her mom. By the end of the day, Sarah felt proud of herself for handling her first period so well.

Meanwhile, Emma got her first period while she was at home. Her mom had already told her about periods, so she felt prepared. When Emma saw the blood, she called her mom, who hugged her and said, "Welcome to the club!" They even had a little family celebration, and Emma's mom gave her a special bracelet to mark the occasion. They discussed what to expect in the future, and Emma felt more confident afterward.

Every girl's experience with her first period is different.

Some girls might feel nervous, while others feel excited. The most important thing is to be prepared and know you're not alone. Carrying a period kit, keeping track of your body changes, and talking to a trusted adult can help make your first period a positive experience. Embrace your period with confidence, and know you have support from those around you whenever you need it.

Choosing Menstrual Products

Choosing the right menstrual product can make your period more comfortable and manageable. There are several options available, each with its unique benefits. Pads are one of the most common choices. They come in both disposable and reusable forms. Disposable pads are made of cotton and have sticky strips to attach to your underwear. They are easy to use and come in different sizes for light, medium, or heavy flow days. To use pads, all you need to do is peel off the backing and stick the pad to the inside of your underwear.

Make sure it's centered to catch the blood. You will need to change your pad every 4-6 hours. Reusable pads are eco-friendly. You can wash and reuse them, which is better for the environment. And reusable pads can save you money in the long run. However, you will need to wash them. Both options can work great, and they tend to be the easiest to use in the beginning.

Tampons are another popular choice. They come in regular and applicator types. Regular tampons require you to use your fingers to insert them, while applicator tampons come with a plastic or cardboard tube that helps with insertion.

The main drawback to tampons is that they require more practice to use properly. To use a regular tampon, wash your hands, then hold the tampon with one hand and insert it into your vagina with the other hand. Push it in until it feels comfortable. For applicator tampons, hold the applicator, insert it into your vagina, and then push the tampon in place with the applicator. Always leave the string hanging outside your vagina for easy removal.

Tampons are small and discreet. This makes them convenient for activities like swimming or sports. However, you must change them every 4-6 hours to avoid risks like Toxic Shock Syndrome (TSS). TSS is a very rare but severe illness that tampons can cause when bacteria get trapped in the vagina. While the chances of getting TSS are very low, it's still a good idea to be careful and follow the directions on the tampon box.

To avoid any problems, just make sure to:
• Change your tampon every 4-6 hours.
• Use the lowest absorbency you need for your flow.
• Wash your hands before and after inserting a tampon.
TSS can sound scary, but if you're careful and change your tampons regularly, you can safely use them. If you ever feel sick while using a tampon, like if you have a high fever, feel dizzy, or get a rash, remove the tampon and tell an adult right away. Tampons can be a convenient and safe option for period care; just make sure to take care of yourself by following these simple steps!

Menstrual cups are becoming more popular, too. They are usually made of flexible silicone. When inserted into the vagina, the cup collects the menstrual blood. To use a menstrual cup, fold the cup and insert it into your vagina. It should pop open and create a seal. You can then remove the cup by pinching the base to break the seal and pulling it out. It's important to always wash your menstrual cup with soap and water before reinserting. A menstrual cup can be used for up to 12 hours and last for years, making it an easy, cost-effective, and eco-friendly option. Period underwear is another excellent choice because it is absorbent and washable. It looks and feels like regular underwear but can hold menstrual blood. Period underwear is convenient and comfortable, especially for lighter flow days or as backup protection.

Choosing the right product depends on several factors. First, consider your flow level. Light flow days might only need a thin pad or a light tampon, while heavy flow days might require a more absorbent pad or a menstrual cup. Comfort and convenience are also significant factors. If you're active, tampons or menstrual cups tend to be more comfortable and less noticeable. If you prefer something simple, pads or period underwear might be the best choice. You can also consider environmental impact and cost when making your decision. Reusable products like menstrual cups and washable pads are better for the environment and can save money over time, while disposable products are more convenient but create more waste.

Real-life experiences can help you decide which product is best for you as well. Jessica prefers pads for their simplicity. She likes that they are easy to use and don't require insertion. She also feels comfortable knowing she can change them quickly if she needs to. On the other hand, Mia finds menstrual cups more convenient. She likes wearing them for up to 12 hours because she finds that it makes them perfect for school days. Mia also appreciates that menstrual cups are eco-friendly and cost-effective. Just like Mia and Jessica, you will find out what products work best for you and your lifestyle.

Finding the right menstrual product can make a big difference in your comfort and confidence during your period.

Whether you choose pads, tampons, menstrual cups, or period underwear, the most important thing is to find what works best for you. Remember, getting used to new products might take some time, and that's okay. You can try different options until you find one that fits your needs and lifestyle (Armand, 2022).

Managing Cramps and Discomfort

Menstrual cramps are something many girls experience during their periods. They happen because your uterus tightens up to help shed its lining, which can cause pain or discomfort in your lower belly, lower back, or thighs. The pain can feel different for everyone. Sometimes, it's a dull ache and other times, it can feel like sharp little twinges. Even though cramps are normal, they can be uncomfortable and make it hard to concentrate on things like school or hanging out with friends.

The good news is there are plenty of ways to feel better when having cramps. One of the easiest tricks is to use heat. A heating pad or a warm bath can make a big difference. The warmth helps relax your muscles and can make the cramps less painful. Staying hydrated and eating a balanced diet can also help with cramps. Drinking lots of water keeps your body hydrated, and eating healthy foods like fruits and veggies can help with bloating and discomfort.

Gentle exercise can also help you feel better. Activities like yoga and walking are great options. Yoga poses like child's pose and cat-cow can help relax your lower belly and back muscles, which eases cramps. Similarly, walking around can get your blood flowing and release endorphins. These can act as natural pain relievers. Plus, you might feel better overall after getting some fresh air.

If the cramps are really bothering you, over-the-counter pain medications like ibuprofen or acetaminophen can help. These can reduce pain and inflammation. Just follow the instructions on the package or ask a trusted adult how much to take.

Another helpful tip is to keep a symptom diary. You can write down when your cramps happen, how strong they feel, and what things help you feel better. This lets you spot symptom patterns and determine what method for relieving symptoms works best for you. For example, you may notice that stretching helps a lot or that drinking extra water makes a big difference.

Relaxation techniques like deep breathing and meditation can also help. Deep breathing exercises can calm your mind and relax your muscles. To practice deep breathing, try taking slow, deep breaths through your nose and your mouth. Meanwhile, meditation can help you focus your mind and reduce stress, making cramps feel less intense.

Understanding why cramps happen and how to manage them can make a big difference in how you feel during your period. With the right tools and techniques, you can reduce your discomfort and continue your daily activities. If you ever have severe pain or symptoms that don't improve with these methods, talk to a trusted adult or your doctor. They can help you find the best solutions for managing your cramps and keeping you comfortable (Scardelli, 2024).

Exercise: Period Tracker Setup

This exercise will help you set up a simple way to track your period and understand your cycle better.
1. Prepare a notebook, calendar, or period tracking app.
2. Mark Day 1: The first day you see blood is "Day 1" of your period.
3. Record Symptoms: Each day, note any symptoms like cramps, mood changes, or cravings. This helps you see patterns each month.
4. Track Flow: Write down if your flow is light, medium, or heavy each day. This will help you prepare for future periods.
5. Count Your Cycle: When your next period starts, count the days from Day 1 of your last period. This number is the length of your cycle (between 21 to 35 days).
6. Review Each Month: Look back and see if you notice any patterns. This can help you feel more prepared for each period!

Period Positivity: Embrace Your Cycle

Let's talk about seeing your period in a new way. Instead of considering it annoying, consider it a sign of your health and growth. Your period means that your body is doing exactly what it's supposed to do. It's a sign that you're growing up and that your body is caring for you. Sometimes, it might feel like a hassle, but it's part of your body's unique abilities.

One way to feel better about your period is to create your period care rituals. Think about adding fun and relaxing items to your period kit that are just for you. Fill it with things that make you feel good, like your favorite snacks and herbal teas that will help you relax. You could add a cozy blanket for those days when you want to curl up and chill. Try doing things that make you happy, like reading a fun book, watching your favorite shows, treating yourself to a hand massage, or painting your nails. These small acts of self-care will help make your period a time of comfort instead of stress.

You can also help others feel good about their periods by promoting period positivity in your community. You can start by talking openly about your period with your friends and family. If you feel comfortable, sharing your experiences can sometimes help everyone feel more comfortable. If one of your friends feels embarrassed or unsure about her period, remind her that it's normal and nothing to be ashamed of (Hartman, 2017). Here are some real-life stories to show how you can make your period a positive experience.

Mia noticed that many girls at her school felt embarrassed about their periods. So, she started a period positivity club to change that. The club meets once a month, and they talk about everything from different period products to ways to deal with cramps. Mia even invited guest speakers like school nurses to teach the girls more about puberty and their changing bodies. Because of Mia's club, many girls started to feel more confident and informed about their periods.

Then there's Sofia, who used to dread her period every month. She decided to flip her thinking and create a self-care routine for her period days. Whenever her period started, Sofia made herself a cup of herbal tea, lit a scented candle, and watched her favorite movies. She also used this time to journal and reflect on the past month. With her new rituals, her period became a time of self-love and relaxation, not stress and anxiety.

Remember, your period is a natural and healthy part of growing up. Embrace it with a positive attitude and take care of yourself during this time. Whether creating your period care rituals, talking openly with your friends, or sharing empowering stories like Mia's and Sofia's, you can

51

help yourself and others feel more comfortable and confident about periods. Celebrating your body's natural process can turn your period into a time of amazing growth and self-care.

Sometimes, life isn't always positive, though. Mood swings can make you feel a bit crankier or more upset than usual. This is a normal part of puberty, and it's okay to feel this way. You might even notice that your mood swings come more often when you're about to get your period. In the next chapter, you'll learn how to manage these mood swings to make you more cool and confident as you continue your path to growing up.

5. MOOD SWINGS
MASTERING THE EMOTIONAL ROLLERCOASTER

I magine you're having a great day, laughing with friends at school, and then suddenly, you feel a wave of sadness washing over you. You can't explain why, but you just want to cry. These sudden changes in your mood can be confusing and a bit scary. But guess what? You're not alone. These emotional ups and downs are a normal part of puberty. Here, you'll learn more about why mood swings happen during puberty and what you can do to help support your emotional health.

Why Do I Feel This Way?

During puberty, your body starts producing more hormones like estrogen and progesterone. These hormones don't just change your body; they can also influence your mood and emotions. You might notice that you feel super happy some days, and other days, you're upset or irritated for no reason.

This happens because estrogen alters the parts of your

brain that control your mood, which is why you might feel upset over something minor. Progesterone, another hormone that affects girls during puberty, can sometimes cause mood swings, too. Together, these hormones can make your emotions feel like they're all over the place.

For example, one day, you might feel on top of the world. Everything seems great, and you're laughing with your friends. Then, the next day, you might feel sad or anxious, and you're unsure why. This is all because of the hormonal changes happening in your body. It's normal to feel a mix of emotions during this time. Many girls go through this. Sometimes, you might also feel extra sensitive and get mad or sad at little things. Many other girls your age go through the same thing. It's important to know that it's okay to have these ups and downs. It's all part of your emotional experience in puberty.

Another way to manage your emotions is by practicing mindfulness. Mindfulness means focusing on the present moment without judging yourself. You can practice mindfulness easily. To start, take a few deep breaths and pay attention to your feelings if you're angry or upset. Ask yourself, "What am I feeling right now?" and "How can I calm myself down?" Sometimes, breathing deeply can help you feel more in control and less overwhelmed by your emotions (Schwartz, 2021).

Emotion Diary Exercise

One way to understand your emotions better is to keep an emotion diary. This process involves writing down how you feel each day and seeing if you can figure out what triggered those feelings. To create your own emotion diary, write down the following each day.

1. **How did you feel today?**
- Did you feel happy, like when you laughed with your best friend?
- Were you feeling sad, like when you got a bad grade on a test?
- Maybe you felt anxious, like when you had to present in front of the class.
- Or excited, like when you find out your family is planning a trip!

2. **What might have triggered that feeling?**
- Was it a conversation with a friend or family member?
- Did a school assignment stress you out or make you proud?
- Did something like a family event happen at home that changed your mood?
- Example: "I felt anxious today because I had a science test, but when it was over, I felt relieved!"

3. **Notice any patterns over time.**
- Do you tend to feel happy after spending time with your friends?
- Are you more stressed when you have a lot of homework?
- Does listening to music make you feel calmer?
- Example: "I feel anxious whenever I have a big assignment, but when I talk to my mom about it, I feel more relaxed."

This exercise will help you understand your emotions better and find ways to manage them. Sometimes, just writing your emotions and experiences down helps you see them more clearly.

The connections between your hormones and emotions during puberty are normal and temporary. Talking to a trusted adult can provide extra support and reassurance if you ever feel overwhelmed. Remember, feeling a range of emotions is okay, and you're not alone.

Managing Mood Swings

When you feel your emotions swinging like a pendulum, it can be hard to know what to do. These mood swings are common during puberty, but there are ways to handle them. One effective way is practicing deep breathing exercises. When you feel overwhelmed, take a moment to breathe deeply. Inhale slowly through your nose, hold your breath for a few seconds, and then exhale through your mouth. This will help calm your nerves and bring you back to a more stable place.

Taking short breaks is another strategy that can make a big difference. All you need to do is step away from what you're doing if you feel emotions building up. Find a quiet spot to relax for a few minutes. This break gives you time to collect your thoughts and regain control. Engaging in physical activity can be helpful as well. Running, dancing, or walking helps release tension and improves your mood. This is because physical exercise produces endorphins, which are natural mood lifters. It's a great idea to find an activity you enjoy and make it a routine.

Building Your Mood Management Toolkit

Creating a mood management toolkit will give you quick access to tools that help you manage your emotions. Here are some ideas to include in your toolkit:

- **Stress Balls or Fidget Toys**: These are great for when you feel anxious or need something to do with your hands. You can squeeze a stress ball when you feel tense or use a fidget spinner or pop-it toy to keep your hands busy and your mind calm.

- **Music Playlist**: Music can have a significant impact on how you feel. Make a playlist of your favorite songs for different moods. For example:
1. Upbeat songs like your favorite pop or dance music can lift your spirits when you are feeling down.
2. Calming tunes like gentle piano music or nature sounds can help you relax when stressed or overwhelmed.
- **Journaling Supplies**: A journal is a great way to work through feelings. Here are a few types of journaling you can try:
1. Gratitude Journal: Write down three things you're grateful for each day to help boost your mood.
2. Drawing Journal: If you prefer, express your feelings through drawing. You don't need to be an artist; just doodling can help you work through your feelings!

Sometimes, despite your best efforts, mood swings can be overwhelming. It's important to know when to seek additional support. If you have persistent feelings of sadness or anxiety that don't go away or have difficulty managing daily activities due to emotional stress, it might be time to talk to a professional. A school counselor or therapist can provide tools and strategies to help you manage your emotions better. They are trained to support you and can offer a safe space to talk about what you're going through.

Whether through deep breathing exercises, taking short breaks, engaging in physical activity, or talking to a professional, there are many ways to manage mood swings. Just find what works best for you and make it a part of your routine. You're not alone in this, and with the right tools, you can handle anything that comes your way (Rapaport, 2024).

Building Emotional Resilience

Emotional resilience is the ability to adapt to and recover from emotional challenges. When things get tough, resilience helps you bounce back. This skill is essential for maintaining good mental health. It means you can handle stress, setbacks, and changes without feeling overwhelmed. Being resilient doesn't mean you won't face problems. It just means you can handle them better.

There are many ways to build emotional resilience. Practicing gratitude is a great method. Simply take a moment each day to reflect on things you're thankful for. This can be as simple as appreciating a sunny day or a kind word from a friend. Writing your reflections in a gratitude journal can help you focus on the positive aspects of your life, even when things are tough. Setting realistic goals is another wonderful way to build resilience. Choose achievable goals and celebrate when you reach them. Each small success will boost your confidence and strengthen your ability to handle challenges.

Another helpful thing to do when building resilience is to develop a positive mindset. You can build a positive mindset by focusing on your strengths and what you can do rather than what you can't. Remind yourself of your abilities and past successes. This positive thinking will help you stay strong during difficult times.

Let's look at real-life examples of girls who have built emotional resilience. Lily faced bullying at school. She felt alone and scared, often thinking, "Why is this happening to me? I just want to feel accepted." But Lily joined a community group focused on kindness and support. This group became her safe space. She made new friends who understood what she was going through. With their help, Lily learned to stand up for herself with confidence. Looking back, she realized that she is stronger now because she didn't give up when times got hard.

Another example is Ava, who struggled with academic stress. She felt overwhelmed by homework and tests, frequently thinking, "I'll never catch up. There's just too much to do!" Instead of giving up, Ava developed effective study routines. She set specific study times, took regular breaks, and asked for help when she needed it. These routines helped her manage her stress and improve her grades. Today, Ava feels proud of her progress and thinks, "I can handle anything if I just stay organized and keep trying." Lily and Ava both showed that resilience can help you overcome challenges and grow stronger, no matter the challenges.

Building resilience is an ongoing process. When building this skill, keep practicing self-care activities that make you feel good. This could be anything from reading a book to taking a walk. Regular self-care helps you recharge and stay balanced. Seeking out new challenges by trying new activities or learning new skills can boost your confidence and resilience as well. These experiences help you learn more about yourself and show you that you can handle different situations.

Like Lily and Ava, you can build emotional resilience by practicing gratitude, setting small goals, and staying positive. Remember, you're strong enough to handle life when life feels tough. Each challenge you face is a chance to learn and grow (Cherry, 2023).

Coping With Stress and Anxiety

Puberty brings a lot of changes, and with those changes often come stress and anxiety. It's common to feel overwhelmed by different things during your pre-teen and teenage years.

Schoolwork during this time can be a particularly big stressor. It's common to worry about getting good grades, finishing homework, or preparing for tests. It's also normal for these academic pressures to make you feel anxious.

Social dynamics and peer relationships also play a role in stress and anxiety during puberty. Friendships can change, and you might feel pressure to fit in a group or deal with conflicts. Changes in family dynamics or new responsibilities at home can add to your stress as well. Perhaps your family is moving, or you're expected to help more around the house. All these factors can make you feel like you have too much on your plate.

As you grow up and life gets more hectic, knowing how to manage stress effectively is important. One of the simplest ways to reduce stress is through mindfulness meditation, which you can learn more about below.

Mindfulness Meditation Activity

Mindfulness and meditation are powerful tools for managing stress. Mindfulness means focusing on the present moment without judgment, and meditation is an exercise designed to calm your mind. Here's a five-minute calm-down exercise you can follow:

1. **Find a Quiet Spot**: Sit somewhere comfy where no one will bother you. You can sit on the floor or on a chair—whatever feels best.
2. **Close Your Eyes and Breathe Deeply**: Close your eyes. Take a big breath through your nose and count to four, then breathe out through your mouth and count to four. Do this a few times. Think to yourself, "I'm letting go of stress with each breath."
3. **Relax Your Body**: Notice how your body feels. Are your shoulders tight, or is your jaw clenched? Take a deep breath and try to relax those spots. Picture yourself

melting into your seat, getting more and more relaxed.

4. **Pay Attention to What's Around You**: With your eyes still closed, listen to the sounds around you. Maybe you hear birds or a fan. Notice the smells or how your clothes feel on your skin. Just pay attention without overthinking about it.

5. **Let Thoughts Float Away**: If thoughts pop into your head, like about homework or something you're worried about, that's okay! Imagine each thought as a cloud drifting by in the sky. Watch it float away without getting stuck on it. Remind yourself, "I can let my thoughts go for now."

6. **Take a Final Deep Breath and Open Your Eyes**: After a few minutes, take one more big breath in and out. Slowly open your eyes and stretch. You're now calm and ready to go.

Another helpful tip is learning how to manage your time better. Sometimes, it feels like there's too much to do, but planning can help. Try creating a schedule where you set aside time for homework but also include time for fun and relaxing activities. By sticking to a routine, you'll avoid doing everything at the last minute and stressing yourself out.

For example, let's say you have a big test coming up. Instead of waiting until the night before to study, try breaking your study time into small chunks each day throughout the week. This way, you won't feel so rushed, and you'll feel more prepared. Balancing your time between schoolwork and fun activities will also help you feel more in control and less anxious.

Sometimes, despite trying these techniques, stress and anxiety can still feel overwhelming. It's important to recognize when you might need help. Persistent worry or panic are signs of needing to talk to someone. Physical symptoms like headaches or stomachaches related to anxiety should also be taken seriously. Talking to a school counselor

or mental health professional can support you. They can offer useful strategies and tools to help you cope better.

Understanding and managing everyday stressors can significantly affect how you feel. Schoolwork, social dynamics, and family changes are all parts of life when getting older. Learning to manage these stressors with practical techniques like mindfulness, deep breathing, and time management will help you feel more confident and in control of your life. If stress and anxiety become too much, don't hesitate to seek help. There are people who care about you and want to support you through these challenges (Kubala, 2018).

Practicing Self-Love and Kindness

During puberty, it's easy to feel unsure about yourself because your body and emotions are going through lots of changes. That's why learning to love and be kind to yourself during this time is so important. Feeling confused or frustrated is normal, but building a positive self-image can help you feel happier and more confident.

Sometimes, you might be pretty hard on yourself, especially when comparing yourself to others. Maybe you've thought, "I wish I looked like her," or "Why am I not as good at this as they are?" These thoughts can easily make you feel down. But here's the thing—no one is perfect. Everyone has their own unique strengths and sources of beauty. Being kind to yourself and reducing those negative thoughts can make a big difference in boosting your self-esteem.

A great way to start is by practicing self-love every day. Try looking in the mirror each morning and saying something nice to yourself. It could be something like, "I am strong," "I am brave," or "I am unique." Whatever positive thought that comes to your mind works. Even if it feels a little weird initially, saying these things out loud can help you feel more

optimistic. Think of it like complimenting yourself each day!

Activities that make you happy are also great ways to practice self-love. Whether drawing, reading a good book, or playing your favorite sport, doing things you enjoy can boost your mood and make you feel good about yourself. Making time for things that bring you joy is important, especially when life feels stressful or overwhelming.

Being kind to yourself becomes even more essential when you're having a tough day. Creating a self-care routine can help with this. Your self-care routine can include taking a warm bath, listening to your favorite music, or spending some quiet time journaling. Doing little things that help you relax can make you feel better about yourself overall. Sometimes, we all need to just chill and recharge. Don't feel guilty about resting; it's just a way to care for yourself.

The people around you also greatly influence how you feel about yourself. Think about how you feel after spending time with certain people. Do they make you feel happy and confident? If someone brings you down or makes you feel bad, stepping back and spending less time with them is okay. It's also a good idea to surround yourself with friends and family who make you feel good and support you. Focus on

relationships that lift you and remind you how amazing you are.

Practicing self-love means making choices that are good for you. Speak kindly to yourself, do things that make you happy, and surround yourself with positive influences. These practices will help you feel happier and more confident during puberty. Remember, you deserve to be loved and treated with kindness, especially by yourself (Moore, 2019).

Journaling for Emotional Health

Journaling can be a powerful way to manage your emotions. Writing your thoughts and feelings safely and privately can help you better understand what you're going through. Writing out your emotions can also help make them feel more manageable. It also allows you to see patterns in your feelings over time. You might notice that certain events or people make you happy while others make you feel stressed. Recognizing these patterns will help you make better choices and take control of your emotions.

Ready to try journaling? Here are some fun ideas to help you get started. Answer the following prompts as honestly as you can.

- Think about a time you felt super happy. What happened? Why was it such a great moment?
- Write about something that's been bugging you lately. How does it make you feel? Why?
- List three things you're thankful for today. It could be anything—from your favorite snack to a good friend.

These journal prompts can help you get going. As you keep writing, you might find that journaling becomes an easy way to process your feelings and feel better after experiencing negative emotions, anxiety, or stress!

Making journaling fun and engaging will help you stick with it. I personally like to draw pictures or doodles that represent my feelings. Visuals can be a great way to express emotions that are hard to describe. You can also create a mood tracker to record how you feel each day. Use different colors or symbols to represent different emotions. This can help you see how your mood changes and what might affect it. You can also write poems or short stories based on your feelings. Being creative will make journaling more enjoyable and meaningful!

Consistency is key to getting the most out of journaling. Set aside a few minutes to write in your journal daily or weekly. It doesn't have to be long. Even a few sentences can make a difference! Use your journal as a tool to reflect on your experiences and emotions. Look back on what you've written to see how you've grown and what you've learned (Montjoye, 2023).

As you continue exploring your emotional health, remember these tools and practices are designed to support you. They help you understand and manage your feelings better. In the next chapter, we'll talk about friendships, crushes, and new connections, and how they play a role in your life during puberty.

MAKE A DIFFERENCE WITH YOUR REVIEW!

"Be kind, for everyone you meet is fighting a hard battle."
— Ian Maclaren

Puberty can be tough. We're all in this together, and your kindness can make a real difference. Imagine someone just like you, who's feeling confused and maybe a little scared about all the changes happening. They want answers but aren't sure where to look. That's why *The Tween Girl's Puberty Bible* exists—to help every girl feel empowered and ready for this adventure called growing up. And you can help.

I have a simple question for you ...

Would you help someone you've never met, just to make their puberty experience a little easier?

Who are these people? They're just like you, or maybe like you were before you started reading this book—feeling unsure but wanting to learn. Our mission with this book is to make puberty less overwhelming for every tween girl out there. The best way to do that is to reach as many readers as possible.

This is where you come in. We all know that people often decide what to read based on reviews. Your review could help another girl, somewhere out there, feel less alone.

Your words might help another girl:
- feel brave about her first period
- feel proud of the changes in her body
- understand that she's not alone in her experiences

To make a difference and help someone out, all you need to do is leave a review. It takes less than 60 seconds, but its impact could last a lifetime.

Just scan the QR code below to leave your review:

If you're willing to share your thoughts, then you're the kind of person who helps make the world a kinder place. Thank you for being a part of this adventure. And now, let's get back to growing up—together.

Your biggest supporter,
Innersparks

6. FRIENDSHIPS, CRUSHES AND NEW CONNECTIONS

I magine something for a second. It's lunchtime at school. You're sitting with your friends and chatting about your favorite TV shows. Suddenly, you realize your best friend is more interested in talking about a new video game that doesn't interest you. You feel a bit left out and wonder why things are different now. Friendships can change during puberty. Understanding these changes can help you manage them better. In this chapter, you'll learn how to support your friendships as both you and your friends grow up and change. You'll also discover all the secrets to starting and maintaining healthy relationships in your pre-teen and teenage years.

Managing Changing Friendships

As you go through puberty, you might notice that your friendships start to change. This is entirely normal. Your interests and activities will likely shift, leading to new experiences and conversations. You might also find that you

and your friends enjoy different things now. You may start to love reading books, while your friend is more into sports. These differences can make it feel like you're growing apart. Still, they can also be an opportunity to learn from each other.

Communicating openly about your feelings is essential to coping with friendship changes. Talk to your friend if you feel left out because your friend has new interests. Let your friend know what you think. You might say, "I notice we're interested in different things now, and I miss spending time together." Finding common ground can help bridge the gap. Maybe you both love movies. Plan a movie night and watch your favorite films together. Discovering new activities to share can also strengthen your bond. Try something neither of you has done before, like baking cookies or playing a new game.

Maintaining old friendships requires effort, especially when things change. When maintaining your friendships, it's a good idea to schedule regular catch-ups or hangouts to stay connected. Plan a weekly or monthly meet-up to chat and enjoy each other's company. Show appreciation and support for your old friends. Compliment them about their achievements and be there when they need a listening ear. A simple text saying, "I'm thinking of you," can mean a lot.

Puberty also presents an opportunity to make new friends who share your interests, which can be exciting. One way to make new friends is by joining clubs or groups that interest you. If you love art, join the art club. If you're into science, find a science group. These clubs are great places to meet people who like the same things you do. Being open and approachable in social settings can also help. Smile and say hello to new people. Ask them about their interests and share yours. You might find that you have more in common than you think.

Friendship Reflection Exercise

Take a few minutes to think about your friendships. This is a fun way to remind yourself why your friends are awesome and how much they mean to you!

1. List Your Closest Friends. Start by writing down the names of your best friends. Think of the people who make you laugh, who are there for you, and who you love hanging out with.
2. What Do You Love About Them? Next to each friend's name, write one thing you like about them. Maybe one of your friends is always kind, another is super funny, or one always cheers you up when you feel down. You can start with:
- "I love that [friend's name] always makes me laugh when I'm sad."
- "I love that [friend's name] listens when I need someone to talk to."
3. Now, write down one activity you love doing with each friend. Here's an example:
- "I love playing soccer with [friend's name] because we always have the best time together."
- "I enjoy baking cookies with [friend's name] because we laugh and get messy!"
4. Reflect on Why Your Friendships Matter. Once you've listed what you love about your friends and the activities you enjoy together, consider how these friendships make you feel. Do they make you happy, confident, or supported?
5. Finding Ways to Stay Connected. Now that you've reflected on your friendships think about how to spend more time with your friends. You could plan a fun hangout with them, write sweet notes to them, or invite them to do one of the activities you listed.

This exercise will remind you about how meaningful your friendships are and help you appreciate the great people in your life. Plus, it can give you fun ideas for staying connected

with your friends in the future.

Understanding that friendships develop during puberty can make these changes feel less scary. It's normal for interests to shift and new friends to come into your life. You can confidently work through these changes by communicating openly, finding common ground, and trying to stay connected. Remember, friendships are a source of support and joy.

Embrace the new connections you make and cherish the old ones. Each friend brings something special to your life; your experiences together are always worth celebrating (DeAngelis, 2023).

Dealing with Peer Pressure

Imagine for a moment that during lunch, your friends discuss skipping the next class to hang out at the park. You feel a knot in your stomach because you know it's not a good idea, but you also don't want to be the odd one out. This is an example of peer pressure. Peer pressure happens when people try to get you to act a certain way or do something you might not be comfortable with. Recognizing the signs of peer pressure is important. You might feel compelled to go along with the group, even if it feels wrong. Experiencing anxiety about fitting in or worrying about what others will think are clear signs of peer pressure.

To resist peer pressure, it helps to practice assertive communication. This means standing up for yourself in a firm but respectful way. For example, if your friends want to skip class, you can say, "I don't think that's a good idea. I'll see you after school instead." Practicing these responses can make it easier to say them when the time comes. You can role-play different scenarios with a family member or friend. This way, you'll feel more prepared when you face peer pressure in real-life situations.

Building self-confidence is also helpful for resisting peer pressure. This is because sticking to your beliefs is easier when you feel good about yourself. Focus on what you value and believe. Consider what's important to you, like doing well in school or being kind to others. Developing hobbies and interests that boost your self-esteem can also help. Maybe you love painting, playing soccer, or writing stories. Activities you enjoy build your confidence and give you something positive to focus on.

Choosing positive influences in your life makes a big difference. Surround yourself with friends who support you and respect your choices. Supportive friendships make resisting negative peer pressure easier. If someone is always trying to get you to do things you're uncomfortable with, that could be a toxic friendship. It's okay to step back from people who don't respect your boundaries. In fact, doing this is a good thing and will probably save you a lot of heartache in the long run. Looking for role models who inspire you is beneficial as well. These could be teachers, coaches, or even characters in a book. Seeing how they handle challenges can give you some ideas on standing firm in your own life.

Sometimes, you might need extra support to deal with peer pressure. Talking to a trusted adult can help. They can offer advice and help you think through your options. Friends who respect your choices can also be a great support system. Find someone who will stand by you and help you make good decisions. Knowing you have someone in your corner can really help.

Trust your feelings about what's right and wrong. If a situation doesn't feel good, walking away is okay. You have the power to make decisions that are best for you. Standing up to peer pressure can be challenging, but I know you can do it with the right tools and support (Hartney, 2024).

Understanding Crushes

Imagine sitting next to someone in class, and suddenly, your heart starts beating faster. You might feel a little nervous or excited whenever they look your way. This is what having a crush feels like. A crush is when you feel a strong emotional and, sometimes, physical attraction to someone. It's a mix of liking and wanting to be around them. You might also think about them often and feel happy when they talk to you. It's a normal part of growing up and can happen to anyone.

Additionally, you might feel butterflies when you see the person you like. Your palms could get sweaty, or you might feel shy around them. You might also want to know more about them, like their favorite hobbies or what they enjoy doing in their free time. These feelings show that you are interested in that person.

Working through the feelings associated with a crush can be tricky. First, it's important to acknowledge and accept your emotions. It's okay to have a crush and feel excited about someone. These feelings are a natural part of maturing. Keeping a journal can help you express your feelings privately. Write down what you like about the person and how they make you feel. This can help you understand your emotions better and sort through your thoughts.

There are healthy ways to deal with crushes that can help you manage these strong emotions. Talking to a trusted friend or family member can help. They might have gone through the same thing and can offer you support and guidance. Focusing on self-care and personal growth is also beneficial. Keep doing the things you love, like playing sports, reading, or spending time with friends. This will keep you grounded and remind you that while having a crush is exciting, your interests and well-being are vital, too.

When and if you feel ready to share your feelings with the person you have a crush on, consider the context and potential outcomes. Think about the right time and place to express your feelings. It might be a good idea to talk to them privately, where you both feel comfortable. Sometimes, the person you have a crush on might not like you back in the same way. It can feel disappointing, but it's important to remember that this happens to everyone. Not all crushes turn into relationships, and that's okay! People have their feelings, and it doesn't mean there's anything wrong with you if they don't feel the same way. When this happens, try not to be too hard on yourself. It doesn't change how awesome you are.

Respecting the other person's feelings and boundaries is still essential, though. If they don't feel the same way, accept their response and respect their space. Everyone deserves to feel comfortable and respected in these situations.

Understanding and managing crushes is an exciting time filled with new emotions and experiences. Embrace these feelings, talk to those you trust, and remember to take care of yourself. Crushes can teach you a lot about your emotions and how to handle them. So, enjoy this part of getting older, and remember that you're not alone in feeling this way (Santos-Longhurst, 2021).

Building Healthy Relationships

Healthy friendships require respect and trust. Respect means you care about each other's feelings and know when to give each other space. Trust is knowing you can count on your friends to be there for you when you need them. Talking openly with your friends is also really important. This means sharing how you feel and listening when your friends talk about their feelings. When you're honest and talk things out, it helps you avoid problems and strengthens your friendships.

Setting boundaries is a critical part of any good friendship as well. Boundaries help protect your feelings and give you personal space. To set boundaries, consider what makes you feel good and what doesn't. What do you need from your friends to feel safe and respected around them? Once you know, clearly tell your friends. For example, if a friend says something that hurts your feelings, you can say, "I don't like being teased about that. Please stop." This helps your friend understand what's important to you and shows them your boundaries.

It's essential to know when a friendship isn't healthy. Unhealthy friendships can happen when someone tries to control what you do, who you hang out with, or how you feel. If a friend acts in these ways, those are red flags. Other signs are if your friend doesn't respect your boundaries or makes you feel uncomfortable. Unhealthy friendships can always leave you feeling bad about yourself or tired. Taking a break or stepping away from friendships that don't make you feel good or respected is okay. Your happiness and well-being matter most!

Building strong, healthy friendships means being supportive and kind to others. One way to do this is to be a good listener. When your friends are talking, pay attention to what they're saying. Ask questions and show you care about how they feel. Celebrate their wins and help them through tough times. If your friend wins an award or reaches a goal, cheer them on and share their excitement. Let them know you're there for them and ready to listen if they feel down. These little acts of kindness strengthen your friendships and show your friends they can always count on you.

Conflicts can happen in any friendship, but handling them respectfully is key. Use "I" statements to express your feelings without blaming others. For example, say, "I feel hurt when you don't listen to me," instead of "You never listen to me." This approach helps the other person understand your feelings without feeling attacked. Finding common ground and compromising can also help resolve conflicts. Look for solutions that work for both of you. Maybe you can take turns choosing activities or find something new you both enjoy.

Being there for your friends when they need you and showing them that you care is essential for maintaining healthy friendships. Doing little things, like sending a quick text to see how they're doing or remembering their birthday, are simple ways you can do this. Doing these things also helps build trust and respect in your friendships. So, remember to be there for your friends, just like you want them to be there for you (Cisneros, 2023).

Celebrating Diversity in Friendships

Imagine sitting at a lunch table with friends from different backgrounds. One friend brings homemade sushi, another shares a story about a festival their family celebrates, and a third friend talks about a tradition from their culture. These moments are special because they let you learn from different cultures and perspectives. Embracing diversity in friendships allows you to see the world differently and appreciate unique backgrounds and experiences. Each friend

brings something valuable, making your life richer and more colorful.

Having diverse friendships means being open-minded and non-judgmental. When you meet someone new, learn about their culture and traditions. Ask questions and show genuine interest. This will help you understand and appreciate their background. You can also invite different friends to group activities to encourage inclusivity. If you plan a movie night or a picnic, invite friends from various backgrounds. This creates opportunities for everyone to share their experiences and learn from each other. It's a simple way to make everyone feel included and valued as well.

Here's a short list of things you can learn about a new culture when you meet a friend from a different background:
1. **Holidays and Traditions** – Learn about special celebrations and what makes them meaningful.
2. **Food** – Try new dishes and discover unique flavors from their culture.
3. **Language** – Learn how to say simple phrases like "Hello," or "Thank you" in their language.

4. **Clothing** – Discover traditional outfits and when they are worn.
5. **Music and Dance** – Explore different music and dance styles unique to their culture.

Celebrating differences in friendships makes them stronger. Participating in cultural exchange activities is a fun way to do this. For example, you could host a potluck where everyone brings a dish from their culture. Or you could plan a day to learn about each other's traditions and customs. Sharing stories, music, and dances from different cultures can be both exciting and educational.

These practices create a supportive and inclusive environment where everyone feels valued and respected. Embracing diversity enriches your friendships and helps you grow as a person. It also teaches you to appreciate the beauty of different backgrounds and experiences. By being open-minded, inclusive, and respectful, you can build solid and lasting friendships with people from all walks of life (Research Outreach, 2020). In the next chapter, we're going to shift back to taking care of your mind and body by exploring how you can develop healthy habits.

7. HEALTHY HABITS = HAPPY YOU!

Imagine waking up and feeling fresh, clean, and ready to take on the day. You stretch, and the sun peeks through your window. Having good hygiene habits makes you feel confident, healthy, and comfortable. They become more important as you get older. After all, you have more sweat and body odor that needs to be taken care of when you enter puberty. Having a daily hygiene routine will help ensure you stay on top of your personal hygiene habits and keep yourself feeling confident. You'll learn how to do that and more in this chapter!

Daily Hygiene Routines

Maintaining good hygiene is crucial for several reasons. First, it helps prevent infections and illnesses. This is because washing your hands, brushing your teeth, and showering regularly remove germs and bacteria that can make you sick. Good hygiene also boosts your self-esteem. You're more likely to feel confident and ready to interact with others when you

feel clean and fresh. Whether going to school, hanging out with friends, or participating in activities, feeling good about yourself makes a big difference. Lastly, good hygiene helps you feel comfortable throughout the day. There's nothing like the feeling of clean clothes and smelling fresh to give you that extra pep in your step.

A consistent morning and evening routine can help you maintain your hygiene habits. It's always a good idea to start your day by brushing your teeth. Use a fluoride toothpaste to keep your teeth strong and healthy. Brush for two minutes, reaching all areas of your mouth. In addition to brushing your teeth, you should floss daily to remove food particles between your teeth. This helps prevent cavities and gum disease.

After brushing, you can wash your face to remove dirt and oil that tends to build up overnight. I recommend using a gentle cleanser that's suitable for your skin type. Next, comb or brush your hair to prevent tangles. If your hair gets oily overnight, you might want to wash it in the morning. Showering regularly is also important. Use soap to clean your body and shampoo to wash your hair. This keeps your skin and hair clean and healthy. Using a conditioner in your hair is also a good idea to keep it looking shiny and feeling soft. You might need to wash your hair more often if you have an oily scalp. If your scalp is dry, it can be helpful to choose a moisturizing shampoo and conditioner.

In the evening, brush your teeth again before bed. This helps remove any food particles and bacteria that have built up during the day. Washing your face at night removes makeup, dirt, and oil. This helps prevent clogged pores and acne. Showering in the evening can also be a great way to relax and unwind before bed. This is a great time to shower if you have busy mornings or just prefer showering at night.

Using deodorant every day helps manage body odor. Select a deodorant or antiperspirant that works for you and apply it to clean, dry skin. Clean and trim your nails regularly to avoid dirt buildup and keep them looking neat. Change your underwear and clothes daily to stay fresh and comfortable as well.

Hygiene Checklist

Creating a checklist can help you keep track of your hygiene tasks. Here's a simple hygiene checklist to help you make sure you don't miss anything:
- Brush teeth twice a day.
- Wash your face morning and night.
- Comb or brush hair daily.
- Shower regularly using soap and shampoo.
- Use deodorant daily.
- Clean and trim nails regularly.
- Change underwear and clothes daily.
- Floss teeth once a day.

Keeping hygiene products in accessible places will make it easier to stick to your routine. Store your toothbrush and toothpaste on the bathroom counter or in a drawer where you can easily reach them. You should also keep your face cleanser, moisturizer, and deodorant in a spot where you'll see them daily. Setting reminders can help you to remember good hygiene habits as well. You can set reminders for yourself by using your phone or a sticky note to remind you to brush your teeth or wash your face.

Maintaining personal hygiene is essential for feeling good and staying healthy. By creating a consistent routine, using a checklist, and keeping products accessible, you will make practicing good hygiene a natural part of your day. Your body and mind will thank you for taking the time to care for yourself (Raising Children Network, 2024).

Fueling Your Body With Good Nutrition

There is nothing better than sitting down to a colorful plate filled with a variety of foods. Imagine for a moment that you have a plate filled with bright green broccoli, juicy red tomatoes, and a piece of grilled chicken. This balanced meal will fuel your body and give you the energy needed to play, study, and grow. Understanding balanced nutrition is essential for keeping your body strong and healthy.

Let's talk about the primary nutrients your body needs. Macronutrients are the big ones. You get most of your energy from carbohydrates, proteins, and fats.

- **Carbohydrates** give you quick energy. Foods like bread, pasta, and fruits are full of carbs that help you stay active and focused.
- **Proteins** help build and fix your muscles. You can find protein in chicken, fish, beans, and even nuts.
- **Fats** are also really important. They give you energy and help your body use vitamins. Healthy fats are in foods like avocados, nuts, and olive oil.

Now, let's talk about micronutrients. Your body requires these vitamins and minerals to stay healthy, even though you only need a little bit of them.

- **Vitamins** like A, C, and D help keep your skin, eyes, and bones strong.
- **Minerals** like calcium and iron help keep your bones strong and make sure that your blood carries oxygen throughout your body efficiently.

And don't forget about water! Drinking enough water keeps

you hydrated, helps with digestion, and keeps your skin looking healthy.

Planning balanced meals and snacks is fun and easy! Start by adding fruits and veggies to every meal. They have lots of essential vitamins that help keep your body healthy. When it comes to grains, try choosing whole grains like brown rice or whole wheat bread instead of white bread. Whole grains give you more nutrients and fiber, which help with digestion and make you feel full longer.

Eat lean options like chicken, fish, or beans for protein. These foods help build strong muscles. While it's okay to have sugary snacks or drinks sometimes, it's better to limit them. They might give you a quick burst of energy, but you'll usually feel tired soon after. Instead, try healthier snacks like yogurt or nuts that will provide steady energy throughout the day.

What you eat isn't the only important aspect of your diet. When and how you eat is essential, too. Skipping meals, especially breakfast, can make you feel tired and unfocused. A good breakfast helps you start your day right. Also, try to eat mindfully by paying attention to how hungry or full you are. Eat slowly and enjoy your food so you can stop when you're full.

Making your meals at home is a great way to control what goes into your food. You can use fresh ingredients and avoid extra sugar and fat in packaged snacks. Plus, trying out new recipes can be fun and exciting! Here are some of my favorite easy, healthy recipes to get you started cooking at home.

Super Smoothie Recipe

Ingredients:
1 banana (sliced)
1/2 cup of mixed berries (like strawberries, blueberries, or raspberries)
A handful of spinach (don't worry, you won't even taste it)
1 cup of yogurt or milk (you can use almond milk, regular milk, or any type you like)

Instructions:
Put the banana, berries, spinach, and yogurt (or milk) into a blender.
Blend on high until it's smooth and creamy.
Pour into a glass, and enjoy your tasty, healthy drink! You can add ice for an extra chill or a spoonful of honey if you like it sweeter.

DIY Trail Mix Recipe

Ingredients:
1/2 cup of mixed nuts (like almonds, walnuts, or cashews)
1/4 cup of seeds (pumpkin seeds or sunflower seeds work great)
1/4 cup of dried fruit (raisins, cranberries, or dried apricots)

Instructions:
Combine all the nuts, seeds, and dried fruits in a bowl.
Mix with a spoon or your hands until everything is evenly mixed.
Scoop the mix into small bags or containers for an easy grab-and-go snack. You can add a sprinkle of dark chocolate chips for a sweet treat!

Healthy Turkey and Avocado Sandwich Recipe

Ingredients:
2 slices of whole-wheat bread
3-4 slices of lean turkey breast
1/2 of a ripe avocado (sliced)
2 slices of tomato
A few leaves of lettuce
Mustard or your favorite sandwich spread (optional)

Instructions:
Lay out the two slices of whole wheat bread.
Spread a little mustard or any other spread you like on one or both slices (optional).
Layer the turkey, avocado, tomato, and lettuce between the slices of bread.
Press the sandwich together, cut it in half if you like, and enjoy a healthy, filling lunch!
Fueling your body with good nutrition helps you feel your best every day. Understanding the role of different nutrients, planning balanced meals, and developing healthy eating habits will help give your body the energy it needs to grow and thrive (Kubala, 2022).

Fun Exercises to Stay Active

You know the feeling you get after dancing to your favorite song? Your heart's beating fast, and you can't help but smile! Staying active is super important for your health and can be a lot of fun. When you move around and exercise, it helps keep your heart strong and your muscles fit. When you exercise, your heart works harder to pump blood, which helps keep it healthy. Strong muscles help you move better and feel stronger. Plus, exercising makes you feel good! When you're active, your body releases chemicals called endorphins that boost your mood and make you feel happier. It's a great way to reduce stress and relax, too. The more active you are, the more energy you'll have during the day. Exercise can even help you sleep better at night.

There are so many fun ways to stay active! One easy option is to dance to your favorite music. You can follow dance workout videos or just make up your moves on your own. Dancing is a great workout because it gets your whole body moving and your heart pumping. You can also try soccer, basketball, or volleyball if you like team sports. Playing on a team is a fun way to stay active and make new friends at the same time. Another great option is nature walks or hikes with your family or friends. Walking outside gives you fresh air and lets you enjoy the scenery while getting some exercise. If you want something more calming, you can give yoga a try as well. Yoga can help make you more flexible while relaxing your mind.

If you want to stay active regularly, you can make and follow an exercise routine. Start by setting small, manageable goals. You can dance for 30 minutes three times a week or go for a walk every evening. Write down your goals and keep track of your progress. Mix up your activities so you don't get bored. You could dance on Monday, play soccer on Wednesday, and do yoga on Friday. That way, you'll work different body parts and keep things fun. Find a time that works for you, like before school or after homework, and stick to it. You'll feel great by staying active and having fun simultaneously!

Staying motivated to exercise can be tough sometimes, but there are ways to help you stick with it. For instance, finding a friend to exercise with can make a big difference. When you have a buddy, you can cheer each other on and have more fun. You could even make it a friendly competition to see who reaches their goals first. Another great way to stay motivated is to reward yourself when you hit your goals. Maybe you will treat yourself to a new book or hang out with your friends after you reach an exercise milestone.

Joining a fun exercise class or an online group can also help. Being part of a group that loves staying active gives you support and keeps you going. Plus, you might make some new friends along the way.

Exercising is a great way to take care of yourself because it supports both your body and mind. Exercise can help you have fun, relieve stress, and feel good about your body. So, grab your sneakers, play some music, and get moving! Whether dancing, playing sports, walking, or doing yoga, staying active is an excellent way to feel your best (Raising Children Network, 2023).

Understanding Sleep and Its Importance

Sleep plays a significant role in supporting your physical growth and development. When you sleep, your body releases growth hormones that help your bones and muscles grow strong.

Getting enough sleep is super important for your brain, too, because this is when your brain organizes everything you learn during the day. This helps you remember things better. For example, if you study for a test and then get a good night's sleep, your brain stores all that information, so it's easier to remember during the test. Sleep also helps with your mood. When well-rested, you're more likely to feel happy and less stressed.

Setting up a good sleep routine is a great way to make sure you get enough rest. A big part of this is going to bed and waking up at the same time every day. This helps your body's internal clock, so it's easier to fall asleep and wake up refreshed. Avoiding screens, like phones and tablets, about an hour before bed is a good idea because the blue light can make sleeping harder. Instead, do something relaxing, like reading a book, taking a warm bath, or listening to calming

music. These activities tell your body it's time to wind down.

Making your bedroom a sleep-friendly environment can help you get better rest. Keep the room calm, dark, and quiet. A cool room helps your body temperature drop, which makes it easier to fall asleep. Use curtains or blinds to block out any light and consider using a sleep mask if you need it. Comfortable bedding and pillows make a big difference, too. Choose

soft, breathable fabrics that feel good against your skin. Reducing noise and distractions can also help you fall asleep and stay asleep. If you live in a noisy area, use earplugs or a white noise machine to block out sounds.

Sometimes, it's hard to fall asleep, and that's okay! Not getting enough sleep can make you feel grumpy and tired, and it can also make it hard to focus in school. If you're having trouble sleeping, try relaxing before bed. Avoid caffeine and heavy meals before bedtime because they can keep you awake. If you're still having trouble sleeping, talk to a parent or doctor. They can help you find ways to sleep better.

Sleep is a crucial part of staying healthy and feeling your best. You can make sure you get the rest you need by understanding the importance of sleep, establishing a consistent sleep routine, creating a sleep-friendly environment, and addressing any sleep issues. This way, you'll wake up refreshed and ready to take on the day (Cleveland Clinic, 2024).

Mindfulness and Relaxation Techniques

Practicing mindfulness can help you relax before bed. Here are some of my favorite mindfulness and relaxation techniques that are perfect for your nighttime routine. The first relaxation technique is called body scan meditation. To do this, lie in a comfy spot and close your eyes. Focus on each part of your body, starting from your toes and moving up to your head. Notice if you feel any muscle tension and try to relax it. This can help you release stress and become more aware of your body's feelings.

Another relaxation practice is mindful walking. When you walk, pay attention to each step. Feel the ground under your feet and notice the things around you. This helps you stay in the present moment and clears your mind.

A third method is progressive muscle relaxation. This is when you tense and then relax different muscle groups in your body. Start with your toes and work your way up to your head. This will help ease physical tension and make you feel more relaxed.

You can also try visualization exercises. Close your eyes and imagine yourself calm and happy in a peaceful place, like a beach or a forest. Some people also listen to calming music or nature sounds, like rain or ocean waves. Try a few different things to see what helps you feel calm, and make them part of your routine.

You can also add mindfulness to your everyday activities. For example, when you eat, try mindful eating. All you need to do is pay attention to each bite, noticing your food's taste, texture, and smell. It can make eating more enjoyable and help you eat slower.

You can take mindful breaks during schoolwork or chores. Just

take a few minutes to stretch, breathe, or sit quietly. It helps refresh your mind so you can focus better. At night, reflecting on positive things from your day is another good practice. Think about three things that went well, even if they're small. This can help you feel good before bed and improve your mood.

Mindfulness and relaxation practices can help you handle stress, focus better, and build emotional strength. Try adding these practices to your day and find what works best for you. Your mind and body will be so thankful that you cared for yourself this way (Hoshaw, 2022). We're going to mix things up in the next chapter by explaining how you can stay safe and positive online and on social media.

8. SOCIAL MEDIA, PHONES, AND STAYING SAFE ONLINE

I magine sitting on your bed, scrolling through tons of photos and videos on your phone. You laugh at a funny meme, like your friend's picture, and maybe even find a new hobby from a cool post. Social media can be a lot of fun, but sometimes, parts of it aren't friendly. Knowing how to use social media safely will help you enjoy it without any worries. In this chapter, you'll learn how to use social media safely, build a positive online presence, and create a healthy balance between screen time and real life.

Using Social Media Safely

Social media does a lot of good things. It helps you stay in touch with friends and family, even if they live far away. You can also share your thoughts, photos, and what's going on in your life with just a few taps. Plus, it's a fun

way to find new interests. Maybe you discover a new hobby, join a club, or follow a channel that teaches you something cool. Social media can help you feel connected and learn new things.

However, not everything about social media is positive. Sometimes, people say mean things online that they wouldn't say to your face. You might also feel pressure to post or act a certain way because of what others are doing. You will also need to protect your privacy. Sharing too much personal information can make you a target for people who aren't safe. It's really important to think about what you post and who can see it for your safety.

One of the best ways to stay safe online is by using your privacy settings. These settings let you control who can see what you post and who can follow you. Make sure that your profile is private so only approved people can see your posts. Additionally, be careful about accepting friend or follower requests. Only say yes to people you know and trust. This will help protect your information, including your passwords, photos, and access to your DMs.

Learn the difference between safe and unsafe interactions. Never share things like your address or phone number online. If someone you don't know starts asking many personal questions or if a conversation makes you feel weird or uncomfortable, those are red flags. It's okay to stop talking to that person and block them if necessary.

Creating strong passwords is another smart way to stay safe online. Your password should have a mix of letters, numbers, and symbols. It also shouldn't be something easy to guess, like your birthday or pet's name. Change your passwords regularly, and don't share them with anyone. This will help keep your accounts and information safe.

Suppose you see something inappropriate, or someone makes

you uncomfortable online. You need to know how to report and block them. Most social media apps have tools for this. If someone is being mean or bullying you, don't respond. Instead, report them to the platform and save any messages as proof. Blocking them will stop them from contacting you again through that account. However, you should still stay vigilant because they could try to talk to you using another account, like a friend's account or an alternative profile. Taking these steps can help you feel more in control of your online experience. Here is a social media safety checklist to help you make your social media accounts as safe as possible.

Social Media Safety Checklist

- Set your profiles to private.
- Only accept friend and follower requests from people you know.
- Never share personal information like your address or phone number.
- Be cautious with strangers who ask personal questions.
- Create strong passwords with a mix of letters, numbers, and symbols.
- Change your passwords regularly, and don't share them with others.
- Report and block users who make you uncomfortable or post inappropriate content.

By following these tips, you can enjoy the benefits of social media while staying safe. Always remember, your safety is the most important thing. If you ever feel unsure or uncomfortable, talk to a trusted adult. They can provide support and help you confidently enjoy the digital world (American Psychological Association, 2023).

Setting Boundaries with Technology

Have you ever spent hours on your phone and then looked up to realize the whole day has flown by? Your eyes probably

felt tired, and you likely didn't get to do the things you planned. This happens to many people, but balancing screen time and other activities can help. One way to do this is by setting tech-free times during your day. For example, you could decide not to use your phone for the first hour after waking up or the last hour before bed. Instead of reaching for your phone, try doing something you love that doesn't involve screens, like drawing, reading a book, or playing a sport. Spending time with family or friends without using devices is also great. These moments bring you closer together, no matter if you're playing a game, cooking, or just chatting.

If you think you might spend too much time on social media, you can use apps to track your screen time. These apps show you how much time you spend on different apps, and you can set limits for yourself. Decide how much time you want to spend on social media daily and stick to it. Turn off notifications, so your phone doesn't buzz every time something happens. That way, you can focus on your work without getting distracted.

Creating phone-free zones in your home can make a big difference. For example, you might decide not to use your phone at the dinner table so you can talk with your family and enjoy your meal. You could have a study area that is a phone-free zone when you do your homework. This will help you concentrate better and finish your work faster.

Talking to your friends and family about your tech boundaries is super important. You can start by letting your friends know about your tech-free times. For example, tell them you won't be available during certain hours but can catch up with them later. When it comes to your family, ask them to respect your phone-free zones. Explain why you have these boundaries and how they help you stay focused and present.

Set expectations for responding to messages. Let your friends know you might not reply immediately, but you'll get back to them as soon as possible. That way, they understand your need for balance and won't expect you to always be online.

Finding the right balance between screen time and other activities will help you enjoy the best of both worlds. When you set limits with technology, you make space for other fun and meaningful things, like spending time with family, trying new hobbies, or relaxing without a screen. If you ever feel like screen time is getting to be too much, remember, it's okay to take a break and reset your boundaries. Your well-being always comes first (Lovering, 2020).

Recognizing Cyberbullying and How to Handle It

Imagine logging onto your favorite social media site, excited to see what your friends are doing, but you see mean comments in your latest post instead. Maybe someone shared an embarrassing picture of you without asking, or you were left out of a group chat where all your friends are. These are all forms of cyberbullying. Cyberbullying is when someone uses the internet or phones to make someone else feel bad or upset. It can happen through mean comments or messages, spreading rumors, or leaving someone out of online groups.

It's important to be able to recognize the signs of cyberbullying. You might feel anxious or sad after using social media when being cyberbullied. Maybe you start avoiding certain apps or websites because they remind you of the hurtful things that were said or done. Changes in your mood can be a sign, too. You might feel sad or angry or lose interest in things you usually love doing. These feelings are normal if you're being bullied online.

If you're being cyberbullied, there are things you can do to protect yourself. First, don't respond to the mean messages. Bullies often want to upset you. Ignoring them can take away their power. Save any messages or screenshots of the bullying so you have proof if you need to report it later. Talking to a trusted adult like a parent, teacher, or school counselor can also help you figure out what to do next. Most apps also have tools to report bullying, which can help keep you safe online.

Support friends who are being bullied. If you see a friend getting bullied online, listen to them and tell them you care. Sometimes, knowing someone is there for you can make a huge difference. Encourage them to talk to an adult who can help. If you feel safe, you can stand up to the bully by telling them to stop. One person standing up can make significant changes. Here's a cyberbullying response checklist to help you act when you see bullying online.

Cyberbullying Response Checklist

- Don't respond to mean messages.
- Save evidence of the cyberbullying by taking screenshots.
- Report the cyberbullying to the social media platform.
- Talk to a trusted adult for support and advice.
- Stand up against cyberbullying behavior if it's safe to do so.
- Support friends who are being cyberbullied by listening and encouraging them to seek help.

Knowing how to recognize and handle cyberbullying will help you stay safe online. If you ever feel unsure or scared, remember you don't have to deal with it alone. There are people who care about you and want to help (Lockett, 2022).

Building a Positive Online Presence

Now, imagine you're scrolling through your social media feed, and you come across a post that instantly makes you smile. Maybe it's your friend celebrating something awesome, like winning a game, or someone sharing an inspiring quote that feels right. These kinds of posts can brighten your day, right? Well, creating a positive online presence is like that, sharing things that make people feel good.

Think about what brings you joy. Do you love baking and want to share a cool new recipe? Maybe you just read a great book and want to recommend it to others. When you post things that make you happy, it makes your profile more attractive and encourages others to celebrate their successes, too. Avoid harmful or hurtful content. Focus on what makes you smile and feel proud.

How you interact with others on social media is as important as what you post. When you see a friend's post, leave a nice comment. You can tell them how awesome their new haircut looks or congratulate them on something great they did. Supporting your friends like this helps build a positive, uplifting community. If you see something you disagree with, it's okay to just scroll past it. Arguing online can create stress that nobody needs. It's better to focus on kindness and positivity!

Now, let's talk about something called digital footprints. This is the trail of stuff you leave behind online, like your posts, shares, and the websites you visit. What you post today could be seen by schools or employers in the future. So, before sharing anything, ask yourself: "Does this represent who I am? Am I okay with anyone seeing it?" If your answers are yes, then posting it is a good idea. However, you should hold off on making the post if you're unsure. It's also a good idea to go back and review your old posts every now and then. If

something doesn't match who you are now or feels negative, it's okay to delete it. This helps keep your online space positive.

Use your social media for good. Support causes or projects that matter to you. Share posts about fundraisers, volunteering, or things happening in your community. It shows that you care and want to make a difference. If you learn something new or extraordinary, you can share that too. It could be a fun fact, a life hack, or something you just discovered. Educational posts can inspire others to learn, and that's pretty awesome. You can use hashtags like #SpreadKindness to join positive movements and connect with people who care about the same things you do.

Remember, your online presence reflects who you are. By sharing things that make you happy, being kind in your interactions, thinking about your digital footprint, and promoting causes you care about, you can create an online space that feels good to visit. Plus, your actions can inspire others and make social media a better place for everyone (Nemours Kids Health, 2023).

As you grow up, you will likely find that you have more questions to ask your parents or other trusted adults in your life. It's great to get some extra help when you need it. In the next chapter, you'll learn how you can talk to the adults you trust in your life without any awkwardness.

9. TALKING TO ADULTS WITHOUT AWKWARDNESS

I magine you have something important on your mind but don't know how to bring it up. Your mom is washing dishes, and your dad is reading the newspaper. You feel a bit nervous about starting the conversation because everyone is busy. But talking to adults doesn't have to be awkward or scary. It can be a great way to get the help and support you need. Here, you'll get some tips and tricks for having conversations with adults as you get older without all the awkwardness.

Starting the Conversation

Talking to adults can be helpful for lots of reasons. One big reason is that they can give you accurate information and advice. When you have questions about changes in your body or feelings, adults like your parents, grandparents, or teachers can give you trustworthy answers. They've also gone through puberty already, so they know what it's like and can share their experiences. This can help you feel less worried and more confident about what's happening to you. Another great reason to talk to adults is that it helps you build a stronger relationship with them. When you're open with your parents or guardians, you create a bond of trust and understanding. They want to support you, but they need to know what's going on in your life to be able to help.

Talking to adults can also make you feel more supported and understood. When you share your thoughts and feelings, it lets them know what's on your mind. Knowing that someone cares about you and is there to listen can make you feel less alone as well. Having someone by your side is comforting, especially when things feel confusing or challenging.

When you're ready to talk, choose the right time and place. Find a quiet spot where you can talk without distractions. This could be your room, a quiet corner of the house, or while taking a walk. Make sure the adult isn't busy and can give you their full attention before approaching them. A good time to talk might be after dinner or when things are calm at home. When both of you are comfortable, the conversation will feel more manageable.

I've been learning about puberty...

Starting the conversation can feel awkward, but having some conversation starters can help. You could say, "I've been learning about puberty and have some questions." This shows you're curious about puberty and ready to talk. Or you could try saying, "Can we talk about something that's been on my mind?" This opens the door to sharing your feelings. If you need advice, you could say, "I need some advice on how to handle [problem]." These simple conversation openers can help break the ice and make it easier to start talking.

Feeling a little nervous about talking to an adult is normal. Letting them know that you are nervous is okay. You can say, "I'm feeling a bit nervous about this, but I need your help." This shows that you still want to talk even though you're anxious. Similarly, you can say, "This has been on my mind, and I want to talk about it." Being honest about your feelings helps the adult understand you better. If you're unsure how to deal with something, help guide the conversation by saying, "I'm not sure how to handle this and could use your advice."

Being open and honest helps build trust and makes your conversations more meaningful. Remember, the adults in your life care about you and want to help. Sometimes, all it takes is starting the conversation.

Active listening is also super important when talking to others. It helps you understand what someone is saying and shows that you care. When you listen actively, you give the other person your full attention. This means looking at them when they're talking, nodding to show you're listening, and waiting until they're done before you speak. Active listening will help you understand their point of view and demonstrates respect for their feelings.

For example, if a parent tells you to spend more time on your homework, you could respond by saying, "I understand that you want me to study more. I'll try to make more time for my homework." This shows them you've listened and are willing to take their advice.

Talking to adults can sometimes feel scary, but it's useful. You can make those conversations easier by choosing a good time to talk, using simple conversation starters, sharing your feelings honestly, and practicing active listening. Remember, the adults in your life care about you and want to help you. Opening up to them can help when you're going through changes and challenges during puberty (Morin, 2021).

Talking to Parents About Puberty

Talking to parents about puberty can feel awkward at first, but it can really help you tackle the challenges it brings head-on. Getting ready for this conversation can help make it easier. Write down your questions or anything you want to discuss. This way, you won't forget what's been on your mind. Maybe you're curious about changes in your body or how to handle your first period. Whatever it is, write these questions down. You can also practice what you want to say to feel more confident. Try talking to a friend or practicing in front of a mirror. Practicing can help you find the right words and feel less nervous. Before talking, take a few deep breaths to stay calm. This simple trick can help you feel more relaxed and ready to open up.

When you're ready to start the conversation, be clear and specific about what you want to talk about. For example, you could say, "I've noticed some changes in my body, and I'm curious about what's happening." This lets the other person know exactly what's on your mind. If you have questions about your period, you could say, "Can you help me understand what's happening with my periods?" Being transparent helps the adult understand what you need and makes it easier for them to give you the right advice. If you're feeling overwhelmed, it's okay to say, "I'm feeling overwhelmed by these changes and need some advice." Being open about how you're feeling helps everyone feel more comfortable.

Listening and responding are essential in a good conversation. Look at your parent or guardian to show you're paying attention. Nodding your head or saying, "I see" shows them you understand what they're saying. If something isn't clear, don't be afraid to ask follow-up questions. For example, if your mom explains how to use a pad, but you're still unsure, you could say, "Can you show me how to do that again?" It's okay to ask! Reflecting on what they say also helps. If your dad suggests using a heating pad for cramps, you could say, "So using a heating pad can help with cramps?" This shows you're listening and helps make sure you understand.

Talking about sensitive topics can feel tricky, but being open makes it easier. If you feel embarrassed, you can say, "I feel a bit embarrassed talking about this, but I trust you." This lets the person know you're shy but still want to talk. If you've read something and want more information, you could say, "I read about this and want to know more from you." It says you're curious and looking for their guidance. If you want the conversation to stay private, you can ask, "Can we keep this conversation between us for now?" This sets boundaries and helps you feel more comfortable sharing. Here's a conversation checklist to help you prepare for a conversation about puberty with your parents or guardians.

Reflection Section: Your Conversation Checklist

- Write down questions or topics to discuss.
- Practice what to say with a friend or in front of a mirror.
- Take deep breaths to stay calm.
- Be clear and specific about your questions.
- Make eye contact and nod to show understanding.
- Ask follow-up questions for clarification.
- Reflect on what the parent says to ensure understanding.
- Express embarrassment or need for privacy.

Approaching these conversations with preparation and openness can make them much smoother. Remember, your

parents or guardians are there to support you. They want to help you go through puberty and all the changes it brings. Being transparent, specific, and honest can make these talks more productive and less awkward. With practice, these conversations will become easier and more natural over time (Sistek, 2022).

Communicating With Teachers and School Counselors

Knowing when to talk to your teachers or school counselors can help when things feel tough at school. If you're having trouble with schoolwork or feeling stressed about your grades, reaching out to them is a good idea. Teachers can offer extra help or give you tips on managing your homework. School counselors also help you find better study habits and handle school stress. They understand that school can be hard sometimes and want to support you.

If you're dealing with bullying or conflicts with friends, that's another important time to ask for help. Bullying can make school feel really uncomfortable, but your teachers and counselors can step in and help fix the situation. They can also give you a safe space to talk about your feelings. School counselors are there to listen if you ever feel upset or worried about your emotions. They're trained to help you work through things and can point you to other resources if you need them.

Talking to a teacher or counselor might feel scary at first, but there are ways to make it easier. Start by asking for a private meeting or email them to let them know you want to talk. This way, they can set aside time just for you. You could say, "Can we talk after class? I need some advice," or "I'm having a hard time with something and could use your help." Being clear about what you need sets up a good conversation.

When you meet with a teacher or counselor, be polite and use good manners. Greet them with a smile and a "hello." Be honest about what's going on, whether it's struggling with a subject or dealing with a personal issue. The more open you are, the better they can help.

Being respectful when talking to your teachers and school counselors is essential. Using polite words like "please" and "thank you" says you appreciate their help. Listen carefully to their advice and tell them you're willing to try what they suggest. For example, if a teacher recommends a new study method, you could say, "Thank you for the suggestion. I'll give it a try." Being honest about your feelings helps them understand what's going on. If you're feeling overwhelmed, it's okay to let them know when you're struggling. You might say, "I'm having trouble keeping up with my homework and could use some help." Showing that you're open to working together makes the conversation go better.

Follow up after your conversation. Check in with your teacher or counselor to let them know how things are going or if you need more help. This shows that you're trying, and they'll likely happily support you. If you're still struggling, don't be afraid to ask for more advice. You could say, "I've been using the study tips you gave me, but I'm still finding it hard. Do you have any other ideas?" Letting them know you're putting in the effort will encourage them to offer even more help. Talking to your teachers and counselors can make a big difference in your time at school. They're there to help you do your best and feel safe. Knowing when to ask for help, being respectful, and staying in touch will help you build strong, supportive relationships with them. Remember, they want to help you through the challenges of school and growing up. Don't be afraid to reach out and ask for the support you need (Avery, 2015).

Seeking Help When You Need It

Sometimes, you might feel like everything is just too much to handle. You might feel overwhelmed, and like there's a heavy weight on your shoulders. These can be signs that you need some extra support. Ask for help if you're having trouble dealing with your feelings or are feeling sad or anxious all the time. Remember, asking for help doesn't mean you're weak. It shows you're strong and brave.

Knowing who to talk to can make a big difference. Your parents or guardians are often the first people you can turn to. They know you well and want the best for you. Teachers and school counselors are also great people to go to. They're trained to help with both school related issues and personal challenges. If you don't feel comfortable talking to your parents or teachers, you can always speak to a family friend or relative. Sometimes, an aunt, uncle, or older cousin can be helpful. You can also turn to community leaders like coaches or youth group leaders. They are there to listen and guide you, too.

Getting professional help is important in certain situations. If you're feeling down, anxious, or stressed for a long time, and it's affecting your daily life, a therapist or counselor can help. They're trained to help you find ways to handle your emotions   and feel better. Talking to a professional is essential when you feel unsafe or are in a harmful situation. They can give you the immediate help you need to stay healthy, happy, and safe. Even if you need ongoing support, seeing a therapist or counselor can make a big difference. They can guide you through tough times and help you feel more in control.

Knowing when to ask for help and who to talk to makes everything feel less overwhelming. Everyone needs support sometimes, and many people in your life care about you and want to help. By communicating your needs clearly and reaching out to trusted adults, you will find the support you need to overcome challenging times. Whether you talk to a parent, teacher, family friend, or professional, the key is to take that first step and ask for help (Nemours Teens Health, n.d.).

Building Trust With Adults

Trust is the key to strong relationships. It helps you feel safe and supported. When you trust someone, you can share your thoughts and feelings without worrying. This is important because it enables you to talk openly and honestly. Speaking freely builds respect and understanding, which makes your relationships stronger and more meaningful.

Building trust takes some work, but it's worth it. One way to build trust is by being honest. If you make a mistake, admit it. It's okay to say so if you don't know something. Honesty shows that you are someone others can count on. Another way to build trust is by keeping your promises. If you tell someone you'll do something, follow through. This shows you're dependable. Similarly, showing appreciation, like saying, "Thank you," when someone helps you, also helps build trust because it shows you value their support.

Respecting privacy and boundaries is another significant part of building trust. You don't need to share everything with everyone. It's important to know what should stay private. For example, it might not be appropriate to share everything from your private life with your teacher because that relationship isn't as close as the relationship you have with your parents. At the same time, respect other people's boundaries and time. Adults have their own lives and

responsibilities, so being conscious of their time and privacy shows that you're respectful. Setting and communicating your boundaries is just as important. Let others know what you're comfortable sharing and what you'd like to keep private. When you respect each other's boundaries, trust becomes even stronger.

Sometimes, conflict happens, and that's okay. It happens to everyone. What matters is how you handle it. Let's say you promised your friend you wouldn't share something personal, but then you accidentally told someone else. In such a situation, the first step is apologizing sincerely to your friend and taking responsibility for your mistake. You could say, "I'm really sorry. I shouldn't have shared that, and I understand why you're upset." A genuine apology says that you understand why what you did hurt them.

After you apologize, show an effort to rebuild trust. Trust doesn't magically come back overnight. It takes time. For example, if you told your friend you'd keep their secret but broke that trust, showing them over time that you can be reliable will help. Keep promises, be honest, and show you've learned from your mistakes. It's also okay to ask for forgiveness and understanding. You might say, "I really want to make things right, and I hope you can forgive me." This shows you care about the relationship and want to work on it. Remember, it's normal to make mistakes, but how you handle them shows how much you value the people in your life.

Building trust with adults is something that happens over time as well. It takes honesty, respect, and effort from both sides. When you have trust, talking openly and feeling supported is easier. This strengthens your relationships and helps you through the ups and downs of growing up (Boys & Girls Clubs of America, 2024).

10. YOUR PUBERTY, YOUR EXPERIENCE
CELEBRATING YOU!

I magine sitting in your room, flipping through an old photo album. You see pictures of yourself from a few years ago, and you can't help but notice how much you've changed. Your hair is different, your body has grown, and your smile is more confident. Puberty has brought many changes. Now, it's time to look back and see how far you've come. In this chapter, you'll take a moment to reflect on the challenges you've overcome, goals you've achieved, and milestones you've passed as you've gotten older.

Reflecting on Your Puberty Experience

Think about everything you've been through and how much you've grown. You might ask yourself, "What have I learned about myself?" or, "How have I changed?" These questions help you understand the changes in your body and feelings and make you realize how much you've grown.

One great way to reflect is by keeping a journal where you

can write your thoughts and feelings about your experiences. Document things such as how your body is changing, how your emotions have been, and what's been going on in your friendships. Over time, this journal will become a record of how far you've come, and it can help you understand your feelings better.

As you look back, consider all the changes you've experienced. Maybe you've noticed that you're growing taller or stronger. Your emotions might have felt all over the place, like a rollercoaster. Sometimes, you were happy, and other times, things just felt tough. Your friendships might have changed, too. Perhaps, you've become closer to some friends while others have drifted apart. All these changes are part of growing up, and they've helped shape who you are today.

Think about your challenges and how you've gotten through them. Puberty isn't always easy. There might have been times when you felt unsure or overwhelmed. For example, when you were feeling unfortunate one day, you decided to talk to a trusted adult or friend, which made you feel better. Perhaps, you started a new hobby, like drawing or reading, to help you relax. Whenever you worked through a problem, you became stronger and more resilient. Celebrate those victories, no matter how small they might seem!

Think about the lessons you've learned. One of the biggest lessons during puberty is understanding the importance of self-care and self-love. Taking care of yourself by doing things like getting enough sleep, eating healthy, and taking time to relax help you feel more confident and happier. Self-love means being kind to yourself and accepting yourself just as you are. It allows you to recognize your worth and appreciate everything that makes you unique.

Another important lesson is learning that it's okay to ask for help when you need it. Having people around you who care makes the tough times easier. Building solid relationships with people who support and encourage you is a big part of getting older. These relationships help you feel like you belong and give you the confidence to face challenges. Reflecting on your adventure through puberty helps you see how much you've grown. It's a chance to celebrate your achievements and recognize your strengths. Keep asking yourself those critical questions and writing your thoughts in your journal. Embrace the changes you've been through and the person you're becoming.

Your path is one-of-a-kind, and every step you take brings you closer to understanding and celebrating yourself. Here's a simple journal exercise to help you get started.

Reflection Journal Exercise

1. **Materials Needed**: Paper, a pen, a needle and thread, and a cover (like a piece of card stock).
2. **Assemble Your Journal**: Fold the paper in half and place it inside the cover. Use a needle and thread to bind the pages together to the cover. (You could skip steps 1 and 2 and purchase a notebook.)
3. **Start Writing**: Use these prompts to guide your reflections:

- What have I learned about myself during puberty?
- How have I grown physically, emotionally, and socially?
- What challenges have I faced, and how did I overcome them?
- What lessons have I learned that I can use in the future?

Take a few minutes each day or week to write in your

journal. This will help you stay connected to your experiences and see your growth over time. Reflecting on your puberty experience is a powerful way to celebrate who you are and appreciate the changes you've gone through.

Celebrating Milestones and Achievements

Imagine waking up one day and realizing you've hit a big moment in your life. Maybe, you just got your first period or started a new self-care routine that makes you proud. These are significant milestones, and they deserve to be celebrated! Recognizing these achievements can make puberty feel like a series of wins instead of challenges.

Making a milestone scrapbook can be a super fun way to celebrate all the big things you've accomplished. You can collect photos, keepsakes, and notes from important moments. You could have a picture from the day you got an important award or a note from a friend who was there for you when you needed it. Writing down your thoughts and feelings about each milestone will help you remember the details and feel proud of how far you've come.

Sharing your achievements with others can be inspiring, too. You could write a blog post, share a picture or story on social media, or talk to a mentor or coach about your experiences. For example, if you've just started a new self-care routine, sharing how it makes you feel could encourage someone else who is going through the same thing. Talking about your milestones can help others see that they're not alone, creating a supportive community where everyone can feel proud of their progress.

Each milestone you reach is a big step forward in growing up. Celebrating these moments helps you see how much you've accomplished and feel more confident. Whether learning to manage your period, building strong friendships, or taking care of yourself in new ways, every milestone is worth celebrating (McNally, 2024).

Embracing Your Future With Confidence

Imagine that you have a blank piece of paper in front of you. That paper represents your future. The possibilities are endless, and you get to decide what comes next. Setting goals can guide you in the direction you want to go. Think about your dreams. Maybe, you want to be a doctor, a teacher, or an artist one day. Write these dreams down. This is the first step toward making them happen.

Next, set personal goals. Instead of saying, "I want to be more confident," you could set a smaller goal, like "I'll practice speaking in front of the mirror for five minutes every day to help boost my confidence." Remember the SMART goals

we talked about in Chapter 1? Taking small steps toward big dreams makes them easier to reach.

Now, close your eyes and imagine your future self. Picture who you want to be in five, ten, or twenty years. Think about the qualities you admire in others, like kindness or courage,

and how you can develop those traits within yourself.
One fun way to do this is by creating a vision board. Find pictures, words, or quotes representing your dreams and goals, and then arrange them on a board. Next, put it somewhere you'll see it every day, like in your bedroom. This will remind you of your dreams and help keep you excited to work toward them.

Another cool activity is writing a letter to your future self. In this letter, you can write about your hopes and dreams. Share who you want to become and the goals you want to achieve. Seal the letter and put it away in a safe spot. You can open it a few years from now to see how much you've grown and what dreams have come true. This will help you stay connected to your goals and remind you of your progress.

Have a positive mindset when reaching your goals. Change and growth don't happen overnight, and there will be ups and downs. But every experience teaches you something valuable. When things don't go as planned, don't get discouraged. Instead, ask yourself, "What can I learn from this?" and, "How can I do better next time?" This will help you stay resilient and keep going, even when things get tough.

Change can sometimes feel scary, but it's also exciting! It brings new experiences, new people, and new opportunities. Embrace it with an open heart and a curious mind. Remember, you have the power to shape your future. Your goals and dreams are totally within reach. You can achieve anything you want with determination, support, and a positive attitude (Perry, 2023).

Resources for Continued Support

This book has been a great resource as you've gone through puberty, but it's about to end soon. Luckily, there are many other resources out there that can help when you have more questions or need extra support. Here, I have included some of the most popular apps and websites that girls just like you love and use to help them work through the challenges they face during puberty.

Some of the best apps girls use today are period trackers. These apps help you keep track of your period, predict when it's coming, and note things like cramps or mood swings. Let's start with the Clue app. Clue is really popular and super helpful. It can predict your cycle based on the info you put in, like when your period starts and how you feel. You can add notes about your emotions or any changes you notice. Clue can help you understand your body better and feel prepared for when your period arrives.

Another excellent app is Flo. Flo tracks your period and gives you amazing health tips. It's also super easy to use. Just log in your symptoms and monitor your cycle. Flo even sends you reminders when your period is about to start or when you need to take medication. Plus, it has educational articles that help explain what's happening in your body.

If you like to keep things simple, Period Tracker is a great choice, as well. It lets you track your period dates and symptoms as well as predict your next cycles without too much extra information. It's straightforward to use, which makes staying on top of your period easy. Furthermore, it's better because it can give you more details and reminders about your cycle.

Using apps to track your period has a lot of advantages over marking it on a calendar. They give you more details and are easier to update, and you can customize them to fit your needs. A tracking app is a great way to feel more in control of your body and stay prepared for what's happening (Blanton, 2023).

Educational websites are useful resources, too. These sites are great for getting reliable information about puberty and can help answer many of your questions. One helpful website is KidsHealth.org. It has guides on everything from how your body is changing to dealing with your emotions. Plus, it's written in a way that's easy to understand, making it a great place to learn about what's going on with your body and mind.

Another excellent site is GirlsHealth.gov. It's focused on helping girls stay healthy and happy. You can find info on puberty, nutrition, exercise, and more. It's a trustworthy source, so you know the advice you're getting is solid. There's also Planned Parenthood, which is a good resource for learning about more complicated things like reproductive health, periods, and birth control. They provide clear, factual information, which can help if you have questions about those topics (Common Sense Media, n.d.).

Taking care of your mental health is essential as well. Puberty can bring a lot of new feelings. Sometimes, it's helpful to have tools that can calm you down or help you deal with stress. The app Calm has guided meditations and relaxation exercises that can help when you're feeling overwhelmed. Whether you're stressed out, having trouble sleeping, or just need a moment to relax, Calm has different exercises, like breathing techniques or calming bedtime stories, that can help you feel better.

Another app that's good for managing emotions is Headspace. This app teaches you how to practice mindfulness, which means learning to focus on the present moment. If you're feeling anxious or having mood swings, Headspace can guide you through exercises to help you stay calm and grounded. It's easy to use and has meditation sessions for beginners. Moodpath is a great app for tracking your emotions. Every day, it asks you simple questions about how you're feeling.

This allows you to notice patterns in your mood and understand what might trigger certain feelings. This can be helpful if you ever want to talk to a counselor or therapist. Plus, it offers tips and exercises to help you manage your mental health (Dorwart, 2024).

If you ever feel like you need extra support, many helplines and organizations are ready to assist you. These helplines are available 24/7, which means you can call or text them anytime you need someone to talk to. Someone is there to listen and give you advice from professionals who understand what you're going through. For example, Teen Line is a great resource that focuses on helping young people with everything from puberty changes to mental health challenges. NAMI (National Alliance on Mental Illness) offers support for kids and teens who are dealing with anxiety, stress, or other mental health concerns (NAMI, n.d.).

Remember, it's okay to ask for help and use these tools to make your experiences with puberty a little easier. You're never alone in this. There are so many people who care and resources out there to support you. These tools are here to guide you every step of the way and help you feel more confident and in control.

CONCLUSION

You've come so far on this adventure through puberty! Let's take a moment to look back at everything we've discussed. We welcomed your puberty experience and all the unique challenges and joys it brings. You learned about what's happening to your body, from skin changes to growing body hair, and how to handle it all with confidence.

We discussed your first period, what to expect, and the different menstrual products like pads, tampons, and menstrual cups. Together, we explored the emotional ups and downs that can happen around your period and how to handle these ups and downs.

We talked about how to keep old friends close while making new ones. You also learned about the importance of healthy habits, like keeping a good hygiene routine, eating balanced meals, staying active, and getting enough sleep.

We covered social media and staying safe online as well. Now,

you know how to set boundaries with technology and what to do if you face cyberbullying. Additionally, you learned how to talk to adults without feeling awkward and build trust with adults when you need help.

Finally, we celebrated your growth, achievements, and how you've embraced your experience with puberty. You've learned the power of self-care and self-love, and how important it is to care for both your body and mind.

From all these chapters, you've learned some essential lessons. Puberty is a normal part of growing up, and it's okay to feel curious, confused, or a little nervous sometimes. Everyone's experience is different; yours is unique.

Now, it's time to put what you've learned into action! Start by creating a daily routine that works for you and use a period-tracking app to help you feel prepared for your cycles. Set boundaries with your devices and spend time doing things you love. Remember to talk to trusted adults when you need help, and practice self-care and self-love daily.

Most importantly, though, remember that you are capable and strong. You have everything you need to handle the changes and challenges ahead. Celebrate your milestones and be proud of how far you've come. Puberty is just one part of your unique life story.

You've got this! Every step brings you closer to becoming the confident, strong person you're meant to be. Keep learning, growing, and celebrating yourself. You are never alone. Many people are going through the same things. Reach out, share your experiences, and support each other.

Your future is so bright! You have the power to shape your path. Trust yourself, stay confident, and keep moving forward. You are ready to face the future with strength and positivity.

Thank you for letting me be part of your adventure. Always remember that you are amazing just the way you are. Keep shining and embracing the wonderful person you're becoming. Your coming of age story is special, and every step is worth celebrating. Keep going, keep growing, and most of all, keep being YOU.

KEEPING THE JOURNEY GOING

Now that you've made it through *The Tween Girl's Puberty Bible*, you have all the tools you need to feel confident, embrace changes, and face puberty with courage. But now, it's time to take it one step further. Help other girls who are just starting out on their puberty experience.

By leaving your honest opinion of this book on Amazon, you'll help other girls find the answers and support they need. You'll be pointing them towards the same help that made a difference for you.

Your review shows other readers that this book is a safe space, a guide to help them understand their bodies and a way to feel less alone. It's your way of keeping the conversation about growing up positive and helpful for everyone.

Thank you for sharing your voice. Puberty can feel less scary when we all help each other, and you're making that possible.

Scan the QR code below to leave your review!

Every review counts, and it keeps the adventure alive for someone else. Thank you for being a part of this!

REFERENCES

Armand, W. (2022, October 5). How to choose period products. Harvard Health. https://www.health.harvard.edu/blog/how-to-choose-period-products-202210052828

Asking for help: Getting past obstacles (For teens). (n.d.). Nemours Teens Health. https://kidshealth.org/en/teens/help-obstacles.html

Avery, A. (2015, April 24). 8 ways parents can help teens with academic overwhelm. GoodTherapy.Org Therapy Blog. https://www.goodtherapy.org/blog/8-ways-parents-can-help-teens-with-academic-overwhelm-0424144/

Bell, S. (n.d.). SMART Goals. Mindtools. https://www.mindtools.com/a4wo118/smart-goals

Best health and wellness sites for kids and teens | common sense media. (n.d.). Common Sense Media. https://www.commonsensemedia.org/lists/best-health-and-wellness-sites-for-kids-and-teens

Blanton, K. (2023, April 28). These period tracker apps will get you in touch with your overall health. Prevention. https://www.prevention.com/health/g43724095/best-period-tracker-app/

Cherry, K. (2023, May 3). How resilience helps you cope with challenges. Verywell Mind. https://www.verywellmind.com/what-is-resilience-2795059

Cisneros, V. (2023, July 10). How to help your teen develop

positive relationships. Outside the Norm Counseling. https://outsidethenormcounseling.com/how-to-help-your-teen-develop-positive-relationships/

DeAngelis, T. (2023, January 13). How to help kids navigate friendships and peer relationships. Https://Www.Apa.Org. https://www.apa.org/topics/parenting/navigating-friendships

Dorwart, L., & Trust, A. (2024, September 13). We tried more than 50 mental health apps to find these 8 winners. Verywell Mind. https://www.verywellmind.com/best-mental-health-apps-4692902

Gupta, S. (2022, September 13). What is self-acceptance? Verywell Mind. https://www.verywellmind.com/self-acceptance-characteristics-importance-and-tips-for-improvement-6544468

Hartman, E. (2017, March 28). So, mindful menstruation is a thing now. Vogue. https://www.vogue.com/article/mindful-menstruation-self-care-fertility-coping-with-cramps-wellness-wmn-space-paula-mallis

Hartney, E. (2024, May 15). Peer pressure takes a toll on mental health—Here's how to deal. Verywell Mind. https://www.verywellmind.com/what-is-peer-pressure-22246

Hormones in puberty. (2021, February). Discover. https://www.yourhormones.info/explore/discover/hormones-in-puberty/

Hoshaw, C. (2022, March 29). What mindfulness really means and how to practice. Healthline. https://www.healthline.com/health/mind-body/what-is-mindfulness

How girls' skin changes during puberty. (2021, April 9). Dr. Zenovia. https://drzenovia.com/blogs/skin-journal/skin-changes-during-puberty

How much sleep do kids need? Recommended hours by age. (2024, June 4). Cleveland Clinic. https://health.clevelandclinic. org/recommended-amount-of-sleep-for-children

Hygiene: Pre-teens and teenagers. (2024, May 22). Raising Children Network. https://raisingchildren.net.au/pre-teens/ healthy-lifestyle/hygiene-dental-care/hygiene-pre-teens-teens

Keeping teens safe on social media: What parents should know to protect their kids. (2023, May 9). American Psychological Association. https://www.apa.org/topics/social-media-internet/social-media-parent-tips

Krisch, J. A. (2022, July 21). Yes, your preteen stinks. Fatherly. https://www.fatherly.com/health/why-preteens-smell-bad-puberty

Kubala, J., & Jennings, K. A. (2018, August 28). 16 simple ways to relieve stress and anxiety. Healthline. https://www. healthline.com/nutrition/16-ways-relieve-stress-anxiety

Kubala, J. (2022, June 20). Healthy eating for teens: What you need to know. Healthline. https://www.healthline.com/ nutrition/healthy-eating-for-teens

Lockett, E. (2022, December 7). What does cyberbullying look like? Healthline. https://www.healthline.com/health/mental-health/cyberbullying

Long, B. C. (2023, June). Body image and self-esteem(For teens). Nemours Teens Health. https://kidshealth.org/en/teens/body-image.html

Lovering, N. (2020, May 1). Family technology rules: How to make boundaries that stick. Psych Central. https://

psychcentral.com/health/technology-boundaries-for-children-and-teens

McNally, M. A. (2024, June 12). From small steps to big wins: The importance of celebrating. Psychology Today. https://www.psychologytoday.com/us/blog/empower-your-mind/202406/from-small-steps-to-big-wins-the-importance-of-celebrating

Miller, C. (2018, December 18). Hair Growth During Puberty. Healthfully. https://healthfully.com/hair-growth-during-puberty-4233546.html

Montjoye, C. D. (2023, October 11). The-power-of-journaling-for-well-being-a-path-to-self-discovery-and-healing. DHW Blog. https://dhwblog.dukehealth.org/the-power-of-journaling-for-well-being-a-path-to-self-discovery-and-healing/

Moore, C. (2019, June 2). How to practice self-compassion: 8 techniques and tips. PositivePsychology.Com. https://positivepsychology.com/how-to-practice-self-compassion/

Morin, D., & Wendler, D. (2021, October 10). How to start a conversation (Without being awkward). SocialSelf. https://socialself.com/start-conversation/

Perry, E. (2023, May 8). How to set goals and achieve them: 10 strategies for success. BetterUp. https://www.betterup.com/blog/how-to-set-goals-and-achieve-them

Physical activity: Pre-teens and teenagers. (2023, February 23). Raising Children Network. https://raisingchildren.net.au/teens/healthy-lifestyle/physical-activity/physical-activity-teens

Rapaport, L., & Goldman, R. (2024, August 28). Mood swings: Definition, causes, and how to manage them. EverydayHealth.

Com. https://www.everydayhealth.com/emotional-health/how-manage-mood-swings-naturally/

Reese, J. (2024a, June 20). The stages of puberty for girls. John Hopkins Medicine. https://www.hopkinsmedicine.org/health/wellness-and-prevention/the-stages-of-puberty-for-girls

Reese, J. (2024b, June 20). What is a growth spurt during puberty? John Hopkins Medicine. https://www.hopkinsmedicine.org/health/wellness-and-prevention/what-is-a-growth-spurt-during-puberty

Santos-Longhurst, A. (2021, February 10). How to recognize a crush—And what to do next. Healthline. https://www.healthline.com/health/relationships/having-a-crush

Scardelli, L. (2024, January 22). 15 things to help with period cramps on days with pain. Verywell Health. https://www.verywellhealth.com/what-helps-with-period-cramps-8413517

Schwartz, D. (2021, March 30). Puberty can be emotionally overwhelming to adolescents. Psychology Today. https://www.psychologytoday.com/intl/blog/adolescents-explained/202103/puberty-can-be-emotionally-overwhelming-to-adolescents

Sistek, S. (2022, October 25). Changes ahead: Talking with children about puberty. Mayo Clinic Health System. https://www.mayoclinichealthsystem.org/hometown-health/speaking-of-health/talking-with-children-about-puberty

Spitza, A. (2016, September 12). Weight changes in kids: Knowing when to act, what to say. Children's Wisconsin. https://childrenswi.org/newshub/stories/weight-changes-in-kids-knowing-when-to-act-what-to-say

Teaching kids to be smart about social media(For parents).

(2023, May). Nemours Kids Health. https://kidshealth.org/en/parents/social-media-smarts.html

The effect of diversity beliefs on friendship formation. (2020, March 5). Research Outreach. https://researchoutreach.org/articles/diversity-beliefs-friendship-formation/

The first bra guide: When and how to buy your daughter's first bra. (2022, June 28). Raising Children 101. https://raisingchildren101.com/the-first-bra-guide-when-and-how-to-buy-your-daughters-first-bra

Vanegas, Y. (2024, May 22). Unlocking teen potential: Tactics for decreasing screen time. Psychology Today. https://www.psychologytoday.com/us/blog/its-not-just-about-the-food/202405/unlocking-teen-potential-tactics-for-decreasing-screen-time

Villines, Z. (2021, January 27). First period: Early signs, how long it lasts, and self-care tips. Medical News Today. https://www.medicalnewstoday.com/articles/first-period

Watson, S. (2018, August 17). Stages of menstrual cycle: Menstruation, ovulation, hormones, mor. Healthline. https://www.healthline.com/health/womens-health/stages-of-menstrual-cycle

Ways to build trust between parents and teens. (2024, September 4). Boys & Girls Clubs of America. https://www.bgca.org/news-stories/2024/September/ways-to-build-trust-between-parents-and-teens/

Wisner, W. (2023, August 29). Everything you need to know about breast development during puberty. Parents. https://www.parents.com/kids/development/puberty/everything-you-need-to-know-about-breast-development-during-puberty/

Youth and young adult resources. (n.d.). NAMI. https://www.

nami.org/your-journey/kids-teens-and-young-adults/youth-and-young-adult-resources/

www.ingramcontent.com/pod-product-compliance
Lightning Source LLC
Chambersburg PA
CBHW060938120626
46557CB00003B/1046